A Woman's Guide to Servant Leadership

A Biblical Study For Becoming A Christlike Leader

Rhonda H. Kelley

New Hope Publishers

Birmingham, Alabama

New Hope Publishers
P. O. Box 12065
Birmingham, AL 35202-2065
www.newhopepubl.com

Library of Congress Cataloging-in-Publication Data

Kelley, Rhonda.
  A woman's guide to servant leadership : a biblical study for becoming
a Christlike leader / Rhonda H. Kelley.
        p. cm.
Includes bibliographical references.
  ISBN 1-56309-434-7 (pbk.)
  1. Christian leadership. 2. Christian women--Religious life. I.
Title.
  BV652.1 .K43 2002
  253--dc21
                                        2001007160

Cover design by Kelly Seward
Series concept by Pam Moore, Steve Diggs and Friends, Nashville, Tennessee

ISBN: 1-56309-434-7
N024113 • 0602 • 3M2

A Woman's Guide to Servant Leadership

TABLE OF CONTENTS

PREFACE

Leadership is certainly a popular topic! Hundreds of secular books have been written about leadership in business. Many Christian books have been published about leadership in the church. Scan the shelves of any bookstore and you will see. Much can be said about why and how to lead.

While God created all people in His image and equal in worth, He gave us a diversity of spiritual gifts. One of those gifts is the gift of leadership. The leadership gift for some people becomes apparent in early childhood—those who are "born leaders"—or leadership may develop over time, indicating that leadership has been taught. Christians believe that leadership ability is from the Lord, a spiritual gift to be used in ministry to others and for the glory of God. And leadership is definitely necessary for the work of the church. God has gifted many men and women for leadership and has given them positions of responsibility. The mantle of leadership is both a tremendous blessing and a demanding challenge.

I thank God for His calling on my life as a leader. Since childhood, I have developed my natural leadership skills. God has opened doors for me to use my gift of leadership. As a Christian, I have sought advice on leadership from the Word of God. I have been influenced by leaders and have seen other leaders emerge as a result of my ministry. God has given me great joy as I lead others, and I pray that He has blessed you for your godly leadership.

You may be wondering why I would write another book about leadership. There are several reasons. This book is not just about leadership; it is about servant leadership as exemplified by Jesus. Secondly, this is an interactive Bible study encouraging the examination of Scripture about leadership. And thirdly, this Bible study is written by a woman for women. The unique perspective of feminine leadership will be reflected. All of these reasons support another book about leadership—a personal biblical study of leadership for women.

Please join me in a dynamic study of leadership. We will define it; we will describe it; we will develop it; then we will dedicate it. We will search the Scripture, seek biblical examples, cite contemporary leaders, and share personal illustrations. I pray that God will affirm your gift of leadership and open exciting doors of service. Though you may face challenges, always remember that the life of a leader can bring immense pleasure and eternal blessings!

—Rhonda Harrington Kelley

INTRODUCTION

Servant leadership has been preached and taught frequently in churches in recent years. However, few Christians have studied the topic personally. This 12-week study, the fourth in the Woman's Guide series, will guide you in your own systematic study of the topic. Background information and biblical references are provided on various aspects of servant leadership. Numerous examples of leaders in Scripture and contemporary life are discussed. However, the impact of this study will come from your own participation. So I challenge you to make a commitment to complete the entire study—to read *all* suggested Scriptures, to answer *all* specific questions, and apply *all* the leadership principles in your own life.

As you begin the study, let me provide a few basic guidelines. They will help you grow spiritually through discipline and dedication.

1. Pray about your participation in this study. Any meaningful study must begin with a heart's desire to grow in the Lord and a commitment to study His Word. This personal conviction must then be expressed in prayer. God will stir your passion for Him and affirm your desire to learn more about Him. Prayer is the key to your spiritual growth. You must pray continually, regularly, and specifically for your prayer to be most effective. During this particular Bible study, pray that God will help you understand your call to leadership and equip you for your role of leadership. Pray for yourself as a leader and pray for others who lead.

2. Set a time and place to do your study. You will complete this Bible study if you set a definite time and place to do your work. Daily discipline is needed for spiritual growth. Determine the best day and time to work on this Bible study. It will also help you to decide exactly how much time you can spend each time you work. (Each lesson should take about an hour.) For some people mornings are good, for others midday is better, and for a few evenings are best. Also, find the ideal place for you to concentrate on your study. The preferred setting will be free from distractions, comfortable, and bright. It might be helpful to identify one place and leave your Bible study materials there for easy access when you are ready to begin. As you establish a routine for Bible study, you will find yourself looking forward to your time and place with the Lord. Try to complete one lesson in one week over a period of 12 weeks so God can teach you effectively about servant leadership.

3. Find some biblical resources. This Bible study book is intended to be the primary resource for your individual use. In addition, you will want to select a Bible translation that is not only accurate but readable. (Biblical quotations in this study are from The New King James Version unless otherwise noted.) You may want to secure several translations for comparison of key passages. I find a Bible dictionary as well as a general dictionary to be helpful. There are many other leadership resources available. Please refer to the selected references in the back of this study. You might explore the Internet for web sites on leadership as well. While resources abound, turn first to the Holy Spirit who will teach you about His Word and servant leadership.

4. Spend time studying the Scriptures. While each lesson will focus on an aspect of servant leadership, numerous Scriptures about servant leadership will be read. Passages from the Old and New Testaments will be included. Read each passage carefully, study its meaning, and apply its truths. Each lesson includes a focal Scripture called "A Leader's Light." These verses are excellent for Scripture memorization. In addition, each lesson includes a section of personal application called "A Leader's Life." Each of these components will help you study and learn God's Word, especially His teaching about servant leadership.

5. Meet with a friend or a small group to discuss the study. While Bible study should be personal, it becomes even more meaningful when shared. If possible, find a friend who will commit to the study and meet with you regularly to share insights. Or you may want to start a small group Bible study on servant leadership. Many existing Bible study groups will choose to use this Bible study as a guide. A partner or small group not only adds depth of meaning to your study, but they also encourage you and hold you accountable. A relationship that builds on shared Bible study is a friendship that lasts forever. Try to meet with a friend or a small group to discuss the study after you have completed your own work. If you are meeting with a small group, see the group teaching guide at the end of the study.

6. Carefully consider each aspect of servant leadership. This Bible study examines 12 different aspects of servant leadership including types, styles, challenges, and blessings of leadership. Each lesson builds upon the next. You will want to finish one lesson before moving on to the next one, and you will want to examine each concept carefully. You may develop an interest in studying more about a particular topic relating to leadership. Don't forget to refer to the bibliography in the back of the book or visit a local bookstore for additional references. There is also a list of leadership quotes in the back of the book. The more carefully you study the topic, the better able you will be to put the principles into practice.

7. Apply the biblical principles of leadership in your life. Reading and studying the Scripture is not enough for the Christian to grow spiritually. You must also interpret and apply the Scripture. During this study, you will search many Scriptures about servant leadership. Try to identify the biblical principle then apply it directly in your own life. A lesson is retained when it is has personal application. You will also benefit from observing how other Christian leaders apply biblical principles of leadership in their lives.

8. Pass on the legacy of leadership to others. If God has given you the gift of leadership, He has given it to you for a purpose. He wants you to share what you have learned with others. Don't keep it to yourself or let it slip away. Instead invest it in the lives of others. Serve them and minister to their needs. You will also want to train them to use their own gifts and abilities. Lead others to lead. One of the best ways to develop future leaders is to include others in serving the Lord with you. God wants you to lead faithfully, but He also wants you to leave behind a legacy of leaders. Your leadership can be multiplied in the leadership of others.

I am confident that the God who created you and gifted you for leadership will create in you great leadership abilities. As a servant leader, you will be a Christlike example in a thirsty world. I will be praying that you will be a faithful servant leader. You will be blessed for your faithfulness. What a joy to know that Christ can live and work through you!

 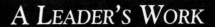

"For even the Son of Man did not come to be served, but to serve, and to give His life a ransom for many."—Mark 10:45

A LEADER'S LIGHT

Think about great leaders in the world and your community. You may think of world leaders—kings or queens, presidents, and prime ministers. Also consider national leaders—senators, governors, and cabinet members. Remember some great local leaders—mayors, city council members, and judges. Identify some Christian leaders—pastors, deacons, and staff members. These leaders have positions of responsibility and influence. They need the guidance of God and the prayers of His people. Write the names of some of these leaders in the margin and commit to pray for them. Pray that God will give them wisdom and courage and strength as they lead.

Leaders have been chosen to influence people toward a goal. While some leaders were born with natural leadership abilities, other leaders must develop their leadership skills. For most, leadership is a combination of both. Leaders face the challenge of becoming the leader God wants them to be—the most effective leader possible.

Personally, I am a grateful leader. I thank God for positions of responsibility He has given me. I am completely humbled by His trust and investment in me. In many ways, I feel that I am a born leader. My mother loves to say that I came out of the womb taking charge of the world. As a child, I accepted positions of leadership at school, at church, and even in the neighborhood. Through these leadership opportunities, I learned how to lead more effectively. Today, as God gives me positions of influence, I try to improve my skills as a leader. Whether born or learned, leaders must strengthen their leadership abilities, or they are not leading like Jesus. *"And Jesus increased in wisdom and stature, and in favor with God and men"* (Luke 2:52).

Do you consider yourself to be a leader? Yes _____ No _____ If yes, what positions of influence are you fulfilling at this time?

Do you believe that you are a natural born leader or a trained, learned leader?

Remember that every person has the power to influence whether or not she holds a position of leadership. You are a leader in your home, church, and community as you influence others.

This lesson will explore the work of the leader—answering specific questions: What is leadership, what is servanthood, and what is servant leadership? Get your Bible, dictionary, and any leadership books ready. Let's try to understand what God calls leaders to do—how leaders can lead more biblically. Continue to pray for yourself as a leader and other people in roles of leadership.

LEADERSHIP

Leadership has been defined in many ways. Each definition gives additional insight into the work of a leader, but there is no one perfect definition of leadership. And there is no one person who is a perfect leader, except Jesus Christ. Read the suggested definitions of leadership below, underlining any key words or phrases.

"Leadership has to do with getting things accomplished by acting through others." (William Cohen, *The Art of the Leader*, p. 3)

"Leadership is more closely akin to nurturing than to ruling; more like guiding than demanding; and more like serving than being served." (Susan Hunt and Peggy Hutcheson, *Leadership for Women in the Church*, p. 40)

"Leadership is knowing *what* to do next, *why* that's important, and *how* to bring appropriate resources to bear on the need at hand." (Bobb Biehl, *30 Days to Confident Leadership*)

"A dynamic process in which a man or woman with God-given capacity influences a specific group of God's people toward His purposes for the group" (Robert Clinton, *The Making of a Leader*, p. 14).

Based on your own knowledge and the definitions of leadership you just read, develop your own definition of leadership. What do you think leadership is?

You should find it helpful to develop your own definition of leadership. While there are good explanations of leadership, a personal understanding will empower a leader to lead more effectively.

Now let's turn to the Scripture for a better understanding of leadership. In Exodus 18, we see that Moses received advice from his father-in-law, Jethro, as he led the children of Israel to the Promised Land. **Read Exodus 18:19-23 and identify some essentials of godly leadership. List in the margin some important attributes of a leader.**

In his wisdom, Jethro encouraged Moses to stand before God, who would guide him through his difficulties (v. 19). A godly leader must depend upon God but lead others with confidence. Leadership includes teaching statutes and laws while living an exemplary life (v. 20). An effective leader enlists others to work together to accomplish God's will (v. 21). A leader bears great responsibility for leadership (v. 22). And a leader can claim victory as God accomplishes His work (v. 23).

Jethro's definition of leadership was simple but profound—biblical leadership requires total dependence on God for guidance to influence others through words of truth and godly example to accomplish God's will. For Christians, leadership begins and ends with God. Now that you have explored the nature of leadership, consider the essence of servanthood.

SERVANTHOOD

It seems quite unusual to follow a discussion about leadership with a study of servanthood. To the world, leadership and servanthood are in direct contrast. But to a Christian, servanthood is essential to leadership. Before one can lead others, one must be fully surrendered to God. Like a slave, a believer has no rights or privileges to call her own; her worth is totally dependent upon the Master.

Jesus taught His followers about servanthood. Though He was God in the flesh, He humbled Himself and served others. Jesus elevated the lowly position of servant to a high position of honor and respect. Remember His encounter with the disciples in John 13? Jesus taught by example how leaders are to first be servants. Jesus Christ, the Savior of the world, filled a basin with water and washed the feet of the disciples. The task of a servant was performed by the Savior who then explained:

"If I then, your Lord and teacher, have washed your feet, you also ought to wash one another's feet. For I have given you an example, that you should do as I have done to you. Most assuredly, I say to you, a servant is not greater than his master; nor is he who is sent greater than he who sent him. If you know these things, blessed are you if you do them."
—John 13:14-17

Who better to teach us leadership and servanthood than Jesus? Throughout His life and ministry He humbly served others. He taught these principles of servanthood to His disciples and He teaches them to us today. To be a leader, first you must serve. To be a godly leader, you must always put others before yourself.

There is an account in the New Testament of a Christian woman who was a servant. **Read about Phoebe in Romans 16:1-2. In this short passage you can learn a lot about the selfless service of one person. What does Phoebe teach you about serving others?**

This unselfish woman was praised by Paul for her service to others. She served Paul himself and other Christians. She lived a godly life and assisted in practical ways. She was a servant to many, not just leading but helping.

The question seems paradoxical: how can a leader be a servant? How can a servant be a leader? But it is not a paradox for a Christian. If Jesus chose to lead by serving, we must follow His example and lead by serving. He embodies for us the process of servant leadership. Though servant leadership is foreign to the world, it is familiar in the church.

SERVANT LEADERSHIP

Leaders in the church look different from leaders in the world. Society dictates that leaders lead by ruling, or giving orders, while the Scripture teaches that leaders lead by serving, or unselfishly doing for others. In his training program titled *Jesus on Leadership*, Gene Wilkes concludes: "Leadership in the kingdom of God is different from leadership in the world. It is still leadership, but those who lead in the kingdom of God look very different from those who lead by the world's standards. Life under the lordship of Christ has different values than life under the lordship of self. Therefore, kingdom leaders are people who lead like Jesus. They act differently than leaders trained by the world. Kingdom leaders are servant leaders because they follow Jesus, who did not come to be served, but to serve" (Wilkes, p. 8).

Jesus the Master Teacher taught His disciples that it was better to serve than to be served—better to be a servant leader than an authoritative ruler. **Read Mark 10:42-45 and let the Master Teacher teach you how to lead as you serve. Fill in the blanks in the verses below to reinforce the instructions of Jesus.**

"Whoever desires to become great among you shall be your _____. And whoever of you desires to be first shall be

_____ **of all. For even the Son of Man did not come to be _____, but to _____ and to give His life a ransom for many."**
—Mark 10:43-45

The greatest leader of all was a servant and challenged His followers to serve others. Jesus wants you to be great, not for your own good alone but for the glory of His kingdom. But the only way to be great is to serve. J. Oswald Sanders said it like this in his book *Spiritual Leadership*:

"True greatness, true leadership, is found in giving yourself in service to others, not in coaxing or inducing others to serve you. True service is never without cost . . . . The true spiritual leader is focused on the service he or she can render to God and other people, not on the residuals and perks of high office or holy title. We must aim to put more into life than we take out" (Sanders, p. 13).

Is that the kind of leader you desire to be? Is that the work you have been called to do? If so, you must look to the Bible, not the world, for examples of leadership. You must let the life of Jesus guide you as you lead. In your home, in your church, and in your community, you can be a woman of great influence as you serve others unselfishly. Servant leadership is not doing everything others want you to do. Servant leadership is accomplishing the task God has given you in a way that nurtures and develops the people around you. Jesus never modeled the first behavior, but He always demonstrated the second.

Reread Mark 10:43-45 to be reminded of the way Jesus led others. List below several specific goals for yourself as you become a servant leader.

1. _____
2. _____
3. _____
4. _____
5. _____

You may want to write these goals on an index card and keep them in your Bible or on your desk as a reminder to serve those you lead.

"[God] has saved us and called us with a holy calling, not according to our works, but according to His own purpose and grace which was given to us in Christ Jesus before time began."
—2 Timothy 1:9

A LEADER'S LIGHT

Are the words of "calling" & "gift" interchangeable

Does God call us according to our gifts?

A call from a loved one is a very precious experience. A telephone call from your husband, your child calling your name, or a dear friend calling with an invitation, all these calls can interrupt the ordinary rhythm of a day and make it very special. For the Christian, a call from God is life-changing. When He calls you by name, you listen. When He calls you to serve, you should obey. God has many ways of calling His children and in this lesson we will explore the nature of a leader's call. Consider some general teachings about the call but reflect personally on your own call.

The Merriam-Webster dictionary gives these definitions of *call*: (1) "to summon to a particular activity, employment, or office" (verb); (2) "an invitation to become the minister of a church or to accept a professional appointment" (noun); and (3) "a divine vocation or strong inner prompting to a particular course of action" (noun). The Holman Bible Dictionary adds this dimension to the definition of *call*: "invitation, summons, commission or naming." Each definition helps us understand that a call is personal and specific. For the Christian the call is from God and is for service.

Read the following Scriptures and identify the type of calling God gives to His children. **Write a word or phrase to describe the specific calling.**

1.	Acts 13:2
2	1 Corinthians 7:20
3.	Galatians 1:15-17
4.	Ephesians 1:15-21
5	1 Thessalonians 2:10-12
6	1 Thessalonians 4:7
7.	2 Thessalonians 2:13-15
8.	2 Timothy 1:8-11
9	Hebrews 3:1-2
10.	2 Peter 1:10-11

God calls all people to salvation (2 Thess. 2:13-15). Male or female, old or young, rich or poor, God wants every person to be saved and spend eternity with Him. God also calls all of His children to holy living (1 Thess. 4:7). Every Christian is to live a righteous, set-apart life. In addition, God calls all His children to serve Him (2 Tim. 1:8-11). While some Christians serve the Lord in full-time ministry, all Christians are called to serve the Lord in some way. God calls some of His children to leadership positions, while all believers have the power to influence others in the name of the Lord. Have you been called by God? How are you fulfilling His call in your life?

Prospective students at the seminary where I teach must testify to their conversion experience and call to ministry. The application form includes a statement of call in addition to other background information. It is the person's conversion and call to vocational service more than grade point average or other credentials that qualifies for admission. The call is important to all believers but essential for ministry.

Paul felt strongly about his call to minister. And he affirmed the call of Timothy and fellow Christians. **Read 2 Timothy 1:8-11 below to understand Paul's perspective on the call.**

"Therefore do not be ashamed of the testimony of our Lord, nor of me His prisoner, but share with me in the sufferings for the gospel according to the power of God, who has saved us and called us with a holy calling, not

according to our works, but according to His own purpose and grace which was given to us in Christ Jesus before time began, but has now been revealed by the appearing of our Savior Jesus Christ, who has abolished death and brought life and immortality to light through the gospel to which I was appointed a preacher, an apostle, and a teacher of the Gentiles."—2 Timothy 1:8-11

God's calling is holy and includes His desire for leaders to be holy! Now let's consider three aspects of a leader's call: a call to close fellowship, a call to human kinship, and a call to servant leadership.

A CALL TO CLOSE FELLOWSHIP

Once a person has accepted Christ as personal Savior, God calls the believer to close fellowship with Him. Isn't it precious that the God of the universe desires an intimate relationship with you? The Christian should have a strong inner desire to know God and to spend time with Him. There is no greater calling than to be a child of God, relating to Him personally.

Christians ought always to take fellowship seriously. Many churches have frequent gatherings with food to visit and build relationships. Fellowship is important to the body of Christ. But close fellowship with God is essential to the spiritual life of the believer. Paul often used the word *koinonia* (Greek for "fellowship") to describe a believer's relationship to the Lord. In 1 Corinthians 1:9, he said: "God is faithful, by whom you were called into the fellowship of His Son, Jesus Christ our Lord." If God is faithful to call us, we should be faithful to fellowship with Him. What a blessing to have a close relationship with Jesus!

Close fellowship with God doesn't just happen. It is like any close relationship. Time, openness, and communication are needed for intimacy. God often uses the relationship between husband and wife to teach about a believer's relationship with Him (Eph. 5:22-27). For a husband and wife to have a close relationship and growing love for each other, they must spend time together sharing openly. I realize this every day in my own marriage. For my relationship with Chuck to grow and for our love to deepen, we must spend time together sharing from our hearts. The hectic pace of life makes that difficult. Chuck and I must work hard to prioritize our time for each other. The effort is worth it as our bond of love grows.

For a Christian to have a growing relationship with the Lord, an intimacy with Him, every believer must prioritize time with God. Prayer, Bible study, and meditation are ways for you to draw closer to the Lord. But it won't just happen. You must seek that close fellowship with God daily as He seeks to be with you. **Take a few moments to consider your present relationship with the Lord. How much time have you spent with Him today? How close is your fellowship with Him? Answer** those questions honestly. **Now spend some time in His presence, knowing Him and experiencing Him. What are some of the blessings of close fellowship with the Lord?**

A daily recommitment to close fellowship with God is necessary for the Christian. It is also natural to follow a discussion of fellowship with God with a study of fellowship with others. Consider the importance of human kinship.

A CALL TO HUMAN KINSHIP

Who are your "kin?" Who are the people you are related to by birth? You may think of your parents or siblings or grandparents or other relatives. Yes, they are your kin. You have a kinship with them, you are family by biological birth. As a child of God, your kin are also other children of God. You have many brothers and sisters in Christ. Some are close kin—believers who are family members, church members, or other acquaintances. But many of your spiritual kinfolk are unknown to you. It is exciting to think about the family of God, His many different children. You are a part of a great family related by spiritual birth.

Just recently a minister friend had the precious privilege of baptizing his eight-year old son, who had publicly professed faith in Jesus Christ. As he baptized his biological son, the father choked up saying, "I baptize you my son and now my brother in Christ in the name of the Father and the Son and the Holy Spirit." As you can imagine, there were few dry eyes in the congregation as the two related by birth testified also to being related spiritually in salvation.

God has called His children to relate to each other in love and kindness. He exemplified close fellowship in His relationship with His disciples. Jesus loved His disciples. He spent time with them and developed special bonds with each of them. His love was not limited to twelve disciples. Jesus loved all people—the old and young, the rich and poor, His followers and His enemies. He desired to have close fellowship with them.

The apostle John began his first-century letter with a discussion of fellowship. He felt strongly about a believer's need to fellowship with God and other believers. **Read 1 John 1:1-7 then fill in the blanks below to complete these biblical teachings about fellowship.**

Fellowship with believers is truly fellowship with the _FATHER_ (v. 3). Those who walk in the _Light_ have fellowship with God (v. 5). Those who walk in the light also have fellowship with _Each other_ (v. 7).
The New Testament discusses fellowship with God and fellowship with others. The word *koinonia* also means relating in love to one another. God calls His children to Christian fellowship. Fellowship with others is truly fellowship with the Father (1 John 1:3). Fellowship is evidence of

walking in the light, of being Christ-like (1 John 1:5, 7). Koinonia expresses the most intimate kind of relationship with God or another person.

Paul longed to have fellowship with the Christians in Rome. His intended visits with them were hindered, but he longed to see them. Romans 15:22-33 records Paul's desire for human fellowship. While his fellowship with the Lord was sweet, he wanted to see the friends who had ministered to him. Fellowship with others brings glory to God but it also encourages the soul of the believer. Paul desperately needed the loving fellowship of Christian friends to refresh his spirit.

God has called you to close fellowship with Him, but He also created you with a need for fellowship with others. Don't be too busy or too distracted to enjoy the blessing of Christian fellowship. There is great personal and spiritual strength from genuine fellowship.

Lesson One examined the definitions of leadership and the description of servanthood. Servant leadership was contrasted with secular leadership. It was determined that God desires His children to be servant leaders. In fact, His call is clear: *"even the Son of Man did not come to be served, but to serve, and to give His life a ransom for many"* (Mark 10:45).

The Bible includes numerous accounts of individuals called to serve the Lord. Let's take some time to remember the call of three of God's choicest servants: Moses, Samuel, and Esther.

Though Moses was not always a willing servant, he was obedient. His story is recorded in the Old Testament book of Exodus. In Exodus 3, God appeared to Moses in a burning bush. **What was Moses' call?** God called him to lead the children of Israel out of Egypt (Ex. 3:10). Though initially reluctant, Moses served the Israelites as leader during their 40 years in the wilderness on their search for the Promised Land. He served his people sacrificially during challenging circumstances. He was a servant leader.

Samuel was another servant leader. An answer to the prayer of his formerly barren mother Hannah, Samuel was dedicated to the Lord before his birth (1 Sam. 1:11). Samuel was raised up in the Lord and heard God's call as a young boy. His encounter with God is written in 1 Samuel 3:4-18. God appeared to Samuel in a vision and called him to serve. In faith, Samuel obeyed His call. **What was Samuel's call?**

God called Samuel to be a prophet, to warn Eli of the judgment on his house (1 Sam. 3:11-14). Though God's command was difficult, Samuel was empowered by the Holy Spirit to do God's will. He humbly served the Lord and the people of Israel as judge, priest, and prophet. Samuel was another servant leader.

Though God did not speak visibly or audibly to Esther as He did to Moses and Samuel, God's call was clear. The orphaned Jewish girl was an

Hold each other accountable.

unlikely leader, but God called Esther to guide her people. During the reign of King Ahasuerus in Persia, young Queen Esther was thrust into a position of leadership. She saved her people from annihilation. Her story is told in the book of Esther. **Based on the details of her life described in Esther 8:1-7, what was Esther's call?**

She was called to save her Jewish people and her guardian uncle Mordecai (Esther 8:1-7). As a result of Esther's servant leadership, the Jewish people lived in peace. Esther was a faithful servant leader.

These examples of servant leaders are inspiring. Can you think of some present-day leaders who serve sacrificially? God uses them in a mighty way as He empowers them to do His work. While they experience some privilege as leaders, they also bear significant responsibilities. **What do you consider to be some of the responsibilities of the call?**

Servant leaders must be godly in character and clear in focus. They are to lead by the Spirit in love and faith. Servant leaders are responsible to God to be holy, obedient, loving and faithful.

Paul summarized the responsibility of leadership in his letter to the church at Ephesus. He pleaded with Christians to live godly lives and serve one another in love. Read the passage below out loud as a commitment to fulfilling your call from God as a servant leader.

"I, therefore, the prisoner of the Lord, beseech you to walk worthy of the calling with which you were called, with all lowliness and gentleness, with longsuffering, bearing with one another in love, endeavoring to keep the unity of the Spirit in the bond of peace. There is one body and one Spirit, just as you were called in one hope of your calling; one Lord, one faith, one baptism; one God and Father of all, who is above all, and through all, and in you all."—Ephesians 4:1-6

It is my prayer that you will be a faithful leader—called to close fellowship, called to human kinship, and called to servant leadership. That is my prayer for myself as well.

A LEADER'S LIFE

Personalize the focal Scripture and apply it directly to your own life. Fill in the blanks below with the words "me" or "my," then read 2 Timothy 1:9 aloud as a commitment to your calling.

God has saved _____ and called _____ with a holy calling, not according to _____ works but according to His own purpose and grace which was given to _____ in Christ Jesus before time began.

Thank the Lord for His grace and calling in your life!

"Where there is no vision, the people perish." —
Proverbs 29:18 KJV

A LEADER'S
LIGHT

A leader has serious responsibility and endless work. As a result, it is essential that the Christian leader has a strong calling from the Lord to serve. In addition to a total commitment, an effective leader must possess qualities of leadership. In their book, *Leadership for Women in the Church*, Susan Hunt and Peggy Hutcheson identify the four qualities that enable a Christian woman to influence those around her to follow God: **vision**, **passion**, **commitment**, and **risk-taking**. While all four traits are important, vision is the one necessary ingredient for leadership. The Bible says it this way: "Where there is no vision, the people perish" (Proverbs 29:18 KJV).

In this lesson, focus your thoughts on the vision of a leader. A visionary leader is capable of influencing the people to do even greater things for God. **What do you think of when you think of vision?**

Vision can be defined in many ways. Merriam-Webster says *"vision is foresight and imagination."* Hunt and Hutcheson say vision is the ability to "focus on possibilities (sometimes called goals or dreams) which guide the decisions and actions of a leader" (p. 38-39). Leaders must be able to envision what *could be* and then pursue the goals to accomplish that vision. My husband, Chuck, defines vision this way: a clear understanding of what God will hold you accountable to do. If that is true, then a leader must have vision to accomplish anything, and that vision will be the measure of success. A Christian leader will stand accountable before God for pursuing the vision given by God.

Vision is not just a term coined by the secular world or corporate America. Vision is a biblical term and a trait of outstanding biblical leaders. Nehemiah was a great leader of the Old Testament. Called by God to rebuild the walls of Jerusalem, Nehemiah was a visionary leader who inspired others to work with him to accomplish a specific goal. His leadership involved both the physical rebuilding of the wall and the spiritual restoration of the people of Jerusalem. **Read Nehemiah 2:11-20 to see evidence of his visionary leadership. Identify the phrase in verse 12 that describes how God defines vision.**

Nehemiah had biblical vision. In verse 12 he refers to *"what my God had put in my heart to do."* He had been called by God to lead his people and given by God a vision to accomplish it. A godly leader must possess the quality of vision but must look to the Lord for His vision for the work. God can place that vision in the heart of the leader. God promises to prosper those leaders who follow His vision (Neh. 2:20).

God clearly called my husband, Chuck, to lead the New Orleans Baptist Theological Seminary then He gave Chuck a vision for the school to accomplish. In fact, Chuck was called by God and received a clear vision of the work before he was ever interviewed for the job. So before Chuck became President he knew his vision for the seminary was to equip leaders to fulfill the Great Commission and the Great Commandments through the local church and its ministries. From that vision God gave him five core values:
1. Doctrinal integrity
2. Spiritual vitality
3. Mission focus
4. Characteristic excellence
5. Servant leadership

The vision from God for our school has given Chuck a clear focus on the task and will be God's measurement of Chuck's faithfulness to accomplish the task.

In this lesson, we will examine specific components of a leader's vision—foresight, imagination, and understanding. As you learn about visionary leadership, identify these qualities in others and develop these qualities in yourself. And remember *"Where there is no vision, the people perish"* (Prov. 29:18 KJV).

VISIONARY FORESIGHT

An effective Christian leader is able to see into the future and project a course of action with the help of the Lord. Foresight not only prevents catastrophe but assists in success. In Scripture prophecy is identified as a spiritual gift, a supernatural ability to foresee the future with the help of God. Many prophets were used by God to warn the people of coming doom or prepare them for the Messiah. In the New Testament, there was a prophetess named Anna who faithfully spoke the words of God. **Read**

her story in Luke 2:36-38. What qualities of leadership did Anna possess?

Do you know what her visionary foresight was about?

Anna served the Lord faithfully in the temple. She was committed to fasting and prayer. Along with Simeon, she received God's prophecy of the coming birth of Jesus Christ. They had great assurance that they would live to see the Savior. The prophecies of Isaiah (Isa. 9:6) and Micah (Mic. 5:2) sustained them. Anna eagerly awaited the Messiah and exemplified for us confidence in God's future plan.

A Christian leader today must have visionary foresight. Through prayer and fasting, God speaks His will clearly to leaders. But leaders must be faithful to pray and be persistent in focus on a desire to know God's will. Then, as Anna did, visionary leaders experience what they have been awaiting. Anna personally met the Savior when He was brought by His parents to the temple. Leaders today see their vision from God unveiled in their lives and work. God faithfully fulfills His promises.

VISIONARY IMAGINATION

An effective Christian leader must have a creative imagination and unusual ability to motivate others to get the work done. There are some amazingly creative leaders today. God has given leaders unique ideas for ministry and gifted them in creative ways for service. Because of God's unlimited knowledge and unbelievable imagination, He has created no two leaders alike, and He has given each leader the ability to think and dream imaginatively. God also directs the thoughts and imaginations of His children who seek Him.

Can you think of some leaders you know who have unusual creative abilities? I can think of several leaders who have fresh, creative ideas and lead in unusual, innovative ways. Each of them gives God the glory for their visionary imagination. Again, I must mention my husband, Chuck. His visionary leadership is often demonstrated in his creative imagination. He often thinks of things that others have never considered. He frequently predicts developments before they happen. While he enjoys thinking creatively, he gives God credit for his thoughts and ideas. Chuck likes to share with me his "wild and crazy ideas." I am always amazed by his unique perspectives and his creative ideas. Often I encourage his ideas, but sometimes I warn him to think about them some more. But always I marvel over his visionary imagination. He embodies this quote by George Bernard Shaw: *"Some men see things as they are and say, 'Why?' I dream things that never were and say, 'Why not?'"*

Do you know who Dorcas was in the New Testament? Though little personal information is known about her, I believe she was a leader with visionary imagination. Read about her in Acts 9:36-43. What did Dorcas do that was so unusual?

The Scripture clearly records that Dorcas was *"full of good works and charitable deeds"* (Acts 9:36). The specific work that she did was unique. When Dorcas saw the need of the widows in her community for clothes, she made them beautiful garments (Acts 9:39). She used her skills as a seamstress and her generosity as a servant to minister in a tangible way. God affirmed her creative leadership. When she died, Dorcas was so mourned that God chose to raise her from the dead through the ministry of Peter. She was restored to life, and many were saved. God can use the visionary imagination of leaders to influence people to Him.

There is a church in New Orleans with visionary imagination. As a part of their ministry to the inner city, they provide two homes in which to train people how to live as a family. What a creative ministry! It is one thing to have as a ministry goal to teach about biblical families, but it is another to do it. God blesses the visionary imagination of His children.

VISIONARY UNDERSTANDING

An effective Christian leader is given discernment by God to understand the mysteries of His will. Though leaders may be innately intelligent and highly educated, true wisdom and understanding comes from the Lord. The wisdom of God allows a leader to make the best decisions and seek the right course of action. Visionary understanding from God goes far beyond human knowledge and is essential to Christian leadership.

The epistle of James contrasts earthly knowledge and heavenly understanding. Read James 3:13-18; then list below the biblical descriptions of both.

Earthly Knowledge   **Heavenly Understanding**

The source of earthly knowledge and heavenly understanding is different. While heavenly understanding comes from God who is all-knowing, earthly knowledge comes from the mind of man. The differences are also evident in a person's conduct. Someone with heavenly understanding lives a pure, peaceable, gentle life of submission. Mercy and good fruits, without prejudice or hypocrisy, are additional characteristics of heavenly understanding (James 3:17). On the other hand, someone with human knowledge is often bitter, envious, and self-seeking, which is earthly, sensual, demonic (James 3:15). A Christian leader must seek visionary understanding from the Lord.

The Woman's Study Bible includes a chart which contrasts these two types of wisdom (p. 1908). It may be helpful to your better understanding of wisdom. The differences emphasize why visionary understanding is so essential to the Christian leader. Read the statements below and write true or false for each statement about spiritual wisdom or visionary understanding. If you are unsure, refer to the Scripture reference noted.

1. Recognizes God as the source of everything (1 Cor. 6:19-20). – T
2. Demonstrates the power of God (1 Cor. 2:5). T
3. Knows the mind of Christ (1 Cor. 2:16). T
4. Submits to spiritual leadership (1 Cor. 14:37).
5. Becomes the servant of all (1 Cor. 9:19).
6. Will last forever (1 Cor. 3:10-14).

A true visionary leader relies on the wisdom and power of God to lead. A true visionary leader knows the mind of Christ and submits to His spiritual leadership. And, a true visionary leader becomes a servant of all. Visionary understanding from God will last forever. Paul, the apostle, understood that heavenly wisdom was the only effective way to lead. He shared his understanding with the Christians in Corinth, and he challenges leaders today to seek spiritual wisdom.

Vance Havner, the great preacher and scholar, once made this profound statement: "A leader has a magnet in her heart and a compass in her head." Wow! That is so true. **What do you think that quote means?**

Why is it so important for a leader to have both "a magnet in her heart" and "a compass in her head?"

Vision is an essential ingredient of effective leadership. Visionary leadership includes foresight, imagination, and understanding. Each of these insights comes from God and should be used by Christian leaders to serve the Lord.

A LEADER'S LIFE

It is impossible for a leader to have a vision for ministry without having a vision for her own life. Do you have a life vision, a purpose statement, a mission? What is the vision you hope to achieve in your life with the help of the Lord?

Now commit that vision to the Lord!

"Be an example to the believers in word, in conduct, in love, in spirit, in faith, in purity."
—1 Timothy 4:12b

A LEADER'S LIGHT

Does character matter? Does a leader's lifestyle affect her leadership? Yes. While many people in the world would say character does not matter, the Bible says that the integrity of the leader matters tremendously. The leader's personal character, not her leadership skills, determines success in God's eyes. In the book *Character Above All*, presidential speechwriter Peggy Noonan discussed character. She said, "In a president, character is everything. A president doesn't have to be brilliant... he doesn't have to be clever, you can hire clever. You can hire pragmatic, and you can buy and bring in policy wonks. But you can't buy courage and decency, you can't rent a strong moral sense."

Yes, godly character is essential for a Christian leader. **When you think of character, what comes to mind?**

Someone once said, "Character is who you are in the dark." In other words, your character is your very nature, the essence of your being, the personal side of inner being, which is then reflected in actions. Character is "the moral code of personhood; integrity, honesty, patience, courage, kindness, generosity, and a strong sense of personal responsibility" (Bowling, p. 78).

Read the following statements about character and reflect on their meanings as you consider the life of a leader.

"Leadership is both something you are and something you do." *—Fred Smith*

"There is no such thing as a minor lapse in integrity."—*Tom Peters*

"Leading from the inside out is a key component of leadership."—*John Bowling*

"Leadership is intensely personal and public at the same time."—*John Bowling*

"Leadership is the tapestry of integrity of heart and life, words and deeds, thoughts and actions."—*John Bowling*

Now that we have discussed the importance of character in the leader, let's consider how character is developed and maintained. A leader does not live morally and honestly without discipline—personal discipline, mental discipline, and spiritual discipline. The disciplined life of a leader strengthens self, influences others, and glorifies God.

PERSONAL DISCIPLINE

Discipline is "training that corrects, molds, or perfects the mental faculties or moral character," according to Merriam Webster's dictionary. Christian leaders must be self-controlled personally but can also depend on the power of the Holy Spirit. In his first letter to Timothy, Paul discussed the qualities of a leader. Biblical qualities of leadership are not based on skills but on character. These character traits must be developed through personal discipline.

Read 1 Timothy 3:8-13 and list below some of the personal traits of a leader.

According to Scripture, a Christian leader must be reverent and honest, sober and pure, unselfish and blameless. Then they will "obtain for themselves a good standing and great boldness in the faith which is in Christ Jesus" (1 Timothy 3:13). But how can a leader remain reverent, honest, sober and pure? With the help of the Holy Spirit and personal discipline, a leader can maintain godly character.

As a leader, you must decide to be disciplined personally and then do it. The personal discipline of a leader should be developed in several areas—including the physical and social. (Other areas of self-discipline will be discussed in following sections.) Physical discipline includes attention to appearance, nutrition, fitness, and health. Social discipline includes focus on marriage, family, friends, and acquaintances. Care of the body and development of relationships are essential to personal discipline. A leader who does not care for herself and her family will not be effective in leadership. Paul included in his list of qualifications for leadership discipline of self and development of interpersonal relationships.

How disciplined are you physically and socially? Set some goals for yourself in each of these areas then be disciplined personally. Remember that your godly character will influence others profoundly. Paul said it this way, "be an example to the believers in word, in conduct, in love, in spirit, in faith, in purity" (1 Timothy 4:12). How can you develop a life that is godly? Paul answered that question later, in 1 Timothy 4. To maintain personal discipline, a leader must (1) give attention to reading, exhortation, and doctrine; (2) not neglect the gift given by God; (3) meditate on the teachings of God; (4) take heed to personal life and doctrine; and (5) continue in doctrine and godly living (1 Timothy 4:13-16). When a leader lives a godly life she will strengthen herself and those she leads. Personal discipline is essential to leadership.

A leader's character does affect her ability to lead. Therefore, a leader must learn to be disciplined personally in order to succeed. Personal discipline in the areas of physical health and social relationships are necessary. In addition, a leader must be disciplined mentally. The gospels report that Jesus "increased in wisdom and stature, and in favor with God and men" (Luke 2:52). Mental growth not only benefits the leader personally, but it also helps the leader accomplish her vision.

Jesus, who was God incarnate, increased in wisdom. Though He was the Son of God, Jesus as the Son of Man continued to learn and grow mentally. Mental growth only takes place through discipline. Are you continuing to learn? Is your mind expanding with new information? Reading is a primary source of mental growth. A person can gain information and insight through reading. We live in such a hectic, busy world, however, that many leaders do not have time to read. Without the intake of information through good books, the mind will stagnate and will not expand. The Bible is a Christian leader's primary textbook for life. There are also many excellent Christian books on leadership. There are hundreds of secular books on the topic. A leader must make time for reading.

In addition to reading, mental growth can result from training conferences, through "think time," and by experience. Information today is available at the fingertips via the computer and the Internet. There is a vast amount of knowledge to be absorbed. Leaders must continue to learn and stimulate their followers to learn.

My husband recently challenged his administrative team to read a very deep, philosophical book (*Avatars of the Word* by James O'Donnell). While they complained about the difficult reading and the high-level vocabulary, they were stimulated by their discussion of the book. Reading

MENTAL DISCIPLINE

a book along with another person can allow exchange of ideas. How mentally stimulating!

Another reason for mental discipline is to protect the mind from false teachings. Scripture warns Christians to guard the mind. Proverbs 23:7 says, "For as he thinks in his heart, so is he." The mind is the control center of life, thus the Christian mind must stay pure and holy as well as increase in wisdom and understanding. What a fine balance—to grow mentally but maintain pure and holy thoughts.

Jesus talked to the Pharisees about the mind, a person's thought life. They were more concerned about outward behavior, while Jesus was concerned about the heart and the mind. **Read Mark 7:20-23 and paraphrase the passage in your own words.**

Jesus told His followers that evil thoughts of the heart defile the person and result in evil actions. The Message paraphrases Mark 7:14-23 like this:

> Jesus called the crowd together again and said, "Listen now, all of you—take this to heart. It's not what you swallow that pollutes your life; it's what you vomit—that's the real pollution."
>
> When He was back home after being with the crowd, his disciples said, "We don't get it. Put it in plain language."
>
> Jesus said, "Are you being willfully stupid? Don't you see that what you swallow can't contaminate you? It doesn't enter your heart but your stomach, works its way through the intestines, and is finally flushed." (That took care of dietary quibbling; Jesus was saying that all foods are fit to eat.)
>
> He went on: "It's what comes out of a person that pollutes: obscenities, lusts, thefts, murders, adulteries, greed, depravity, deceptive dealings, carousing, mean looks, slander, arrogance, foolishness—all these are vomit from the heart. There is the source of your pollution."

Christian leaders must guard their thoughts, because what they think will come out of their mouths eventually.

Christian leaders must grow mentally, gaining wisdom and knowledge from many sources as well as life experience. We must also grow emotionally. Emotional health greatly impacts a person's being and affects attitude as well as behavior. God created men and women with feelings and emotions. He wants His children to experience love, joy, and passion. The

Scripture affirms this truth in John 10:10: *"I have come that they might have life, and that they may have it more abundantly."*

A Christian leader must be strong emotionally. That inner strength comes from the Lord and helps us lead with confidence. A Christian leader must be disciplined emotionally to be balanced and healthy. A strong self-esteem, positive feelings toward others, and trust in God are the foundations of emotional health. Discipline of the mind and emotions strengthens a Christian leader to lead more effectively. But above all, a Christian leader must be disciplined spiritually.

Personal, mental, and spiritual disciplines are essential to the life of a Christian leader. If a leader is not growing in each of these areas, she will be unable to lead. A life without growth becomes dry and stagnant. Without daily discipline a leader remains immature in the faith. But spiritual discipline can bring maturity. We are urged in 1 Peter 2:1-3: "Therefore, laying aside all malice, all deceit, hypocrisy, envy, and all evil speaking, as newborn babes, desire the pure milk of the word, that you may grow thereby, if indeed you have tasted that the Lord is gracious."

Spiritual discipline is a continual process that helps a Christian leader mature in Christ and follow God's will. Specific spiritual disciplines must be practiced daily—Bible study, prayer, worship, fellowship, service, and witnessing. Through spiritual discipline a believer is delivered from the power of sin. Without spiritual discipline a believer cannot walk with Christ, grow in faith, or lead others according to God's will.

How long has it been since you studied the fruit of the Holy Spirit? Remember, the fruit of the Holy Spirit refers to godly attributes that result from spiritual discipline. **Read Galatians 5:22-23 and list below the fruit of the Spirit.**

SPIRITUAL DISCIPLINE

A Christian cannot experience love, joy, and peace without self-control. A Christian cannot be patient, kind, or good without being self-disciplined. A Christian cannot be faithful and gentle without spiritual discipline. Self-control is the crowning fruit of the Spirit.

Spiritual discipline produces the fruit of the Spirit in a Christian leader. Spiritual discipline affects the believer's relationship with God, others, and self. Though difficult and challenging, spiritual discipline produces a harvest of righteousness and peace for the one who practices it (Hebrews 12:11).

In the blanks below, write an adjective to describe the fruit of the Spirit in each relationship.

In relation to God
love

joy

peace

In relation to others
patience

kindness

goodness

In relation to self
faithfulness

gentleness

self-control

We discover that the challenge of spiritual discipline is worth it when we experience the fruit of the Spirit. As a Christian leader matures spiritually, she becomes more Christ-like and can lead according to His will. That should be the goal for every Christian leader. But it is a difficult goal to accomplish. With the help of the Holy Spirit, every Christian leader can grow spiritually and develop godly character. In relation to God, we can experience deep love, abundant joy, and lasting peace. In relation to others we can develop enduring patience, tender kindness, and impartial goodness. In relation to self, we can possess strong faith, genuine gentleness, and steadfast self-control.

How can you develop discipline as a leader so that godly character will characterize your life? You can start now and continue throughout your lifetime. The following suggestions may help you develop personal, mental and spiritual discipline as you lead.

1. Set priorities. With the help of the Lord, determine what you should do and what you should not do. Then place those commitments in order of importance.

2. Solve problems. As challenges arise, depend on the Lord to help you figure them out and resolve any conflict. Problems become much bigger if they are not handled immediately.

3. Stick to principles. As a Christian, stick to biblical principles. Let those godly standards guide your actions and attitudes.

4. Submit to practice. Work hard and continue to work; learning comes with experience. As you lead, you will actually become a better leader.

5. Seek a plan. Make knowing God's will your highest aim. Pursue His will through prayer, Bible study, and wise counsel. Once you identify His will, stick to it.

Evaluate your personal life by honestly answering the questions below.

How disciplined are you personally?

How disciplined are you mentally?

How disciplined are you spiritually?

Now that you have honestly examined your own life, set some goals for yourself in these areas of self-discipline. Remember that you cannot lead others unless you are leading a godly, disciplined life.

There is no greater challenge for a leader than the daily discipline necessary for personal, mental, and spiritual growth. But the effort is worth it! The life of a leader speaks much louder than words. The fruit of the Spirit impacts those you lead, and your godly character influences your followers to the Lord.

"And I will pray the Father, and He will give you another Helper, that He may abide with you forever."—John 14:16

A LEADER'S LIGHT

The word "power" conjures up many images in our minds. Unfortunately, most thoughts about "power" are negative because power and position have been so often abused. A person's physical power can victimize. A person's mental power can intimidate. And a person's positional power can thwart the accomplishments of others. Sin has distorted God's gift of power. When used selfishly or to control others, power is indeed a negative force.

But power does not have to be a negative force—it can be positive. Power has the potential to influence people for godliness. In his book, *Leadership: The Inner Side of Greatness*, Peter Koestenbaum says, "Leadership is the use of power. But power, to be ethical, must never be abused. To ensure that, one rule cannot be broken: Power is to be used only for the benefit of others, never for yourself. That is the essential generosity and self-sacrifice of the leader." All leaders should resist abusing their power. Christian leaders, however, must only use their power to help others. Then power is a blessing, not a burden.

What do you think of when you consider the concept of power?

Who do you consider to be powerful in your life?

How has their power helped you or hurt you?

There are people in power at all levels of work and relationships. They have the power to influence for good or evil. As a Christian leader, you will have the power to influence for good or evil. Ask the Lord to help you use your power for His glory.

Power is the natural result of a position of leadership. A president, pastor, or principal wields power because of a position of authority. A friend of ours quickly discovered that his words were powerful when he became president of an institution. He casually mentioned to one of his staff how nice a swing on the porch of his home would be. The next day, there was a swing on his porch! He was shocked. In a very real way, he learned that when the president spoke, the words were heeded. He realized how careful he must be with every word he uttered. There was power in his position.

In this lesson, you will consider a leader's power—its abuse, its source, and its use. The primary focus will be on the power of the Holy Spirit to help the leader accomplish what God has called her to do. See if you change your mind about power, especially its negative impact.

THE ABUSE OF POWER

David was King of Judah and Israel, one of the Bible's greatest leaders. Following Saul's death, David was anointed king. (The book of 2 Samuel records the details of his 40-year reign.) He led the nations politically and spiritually. God made a covenant with David to build his house and use his son to build the temple. Over time David rose to power and his influence was great. Though David was a follower of God, he had a sinful heart. And his sin led him to abuse his power.

Read 2 Samuel 11, which records the sinful downfall of King David. **Fill in the blanks below to summarize the events leading to the fall of this leader.**

_____ **saw a beautiful woman.**
He _____ **her.**
_____ **became pregnant.**
He had _____ **killed.**
She became his _____**.**

That is a simplification of a tragic story that affected all who were involved. David saw a beautiful woman (v. 2). He sent for her and lay with her (v. 4). Bathsheba then became pregnant with the king's child (v. 5). David brought her husband Uriah home from the battlefield in an attempt to legitimize the conception, but Uriah was too loyal to have intimate relations with his wife. David had Uriah killed to try to cover his sin (v. 17). And, Bathsheba became his wife and bore him a son (v. 27).

King David had abused his power. He used his position of leadership to fulfill his sinful lusts. And he paid the consequences of his sin. The son of David and Bathsheba died (2 Sam. 12:18). His sin was passed down to his next generation; David's son Amnon later plotted to rape his lovely stepsister Tamar, another abuse of power. And David suffered from the pain of his son's sin. He was judged personally for his sin. However, David received the forgiveness of God and was restored to close fellowship with God (2 Sam. 24:10-17). David wrote of his repentance and desire for restoration in Psalm 51:10-12: "Create in me a clean heart, O God, and renew a steadfast spirit within me. Do not cast me away from Your presence, and do not take Your Holy Spirit from me. Restore to me the joy of Your salvation, and uphold me by Your generous Spirit." How tragic when power is abused!

Christian leaders today must be warned about the abuse of power. When power is used for selfish or sinful reasons, a leader must be corrected. So be alert to evidences of abuse in your own life and the lives of other leaders. Calvin Miller identified five evidences of power abuse in his book *The Empowered Leader* (pp. 130-133). These can be helpful in recognizing potential abuse by leaders.

1. Giving up those disciplines we demand of "underlings." When a leader stops growing spiritually, she is at great risk of power abuse.
2. Believing that others owe me whatever use I can make of them. Sinful leaders attempt to justify their abusive actions by rationalizing that the abuse was worthy payment.
3. Trying to fix things up rather than make things right. Leaders fail when they try to fix the problems of others and don't confess their own sin.
4. Closing my mind to every suggestion that I could be out of God's will. Blinded by sin, a leader who has abused her power denies her unfaithfulness and hardens her heart.
5. Believing that people in my way are expendable. In an attempt to cover up her own sin, a leader may destroy another person. Christian leaders need to be warned about the human tendency to abuse power.

Unfortunately, the Christian world is not immune from power abusers. There are Christian men and women in positions of leadership who have used or abused those they were called to serve. Power abuse is not right, especially among the children of God. So pray fervently that you will never abuse the power God has given you. Pray that other Christian leaders will not use their positions for selfish gain. If we can avoid taking power into our own hands, God will empower us to do His work according to His will.

THE SOURCE OF POWER

The Holy Spirit is a believer's source of power. God, through His Spirit, empowers the Christian to do His work. Aren't you grateful that you are not the source of your power? You can rejoice in knowing that God gives power to His children at the time of their conversion. And He continually pours out His power to lead, guide, and direct in life. It is important for a Christian leader to realize that before you can be in authority, you must be *under* authority—under the power and control of the Holy Spirit.

The gospel of John focuses on the Holy Spirit as the source of power for believers. Turn in your Bible to John 7:37-39 and read the promise of Jesus to leave His Spirit to empower His followers. Now read the following Scriptures and identify the role of the Holy Spirit in the life of the Christian.

John 3:16
John 7:38
John 14:16
John 14:26
John 16:13

The Holy Spirit ministers to the believer in many ways. First, the Holy Spirit indwells the convert at the time of salvation (John 3:16) then the Holy Spirit flows through His children as living water (John 7:38). He empowers as helper, to strengthen the believer and reveal God's will (John 14:16). The Holy Spirit also serves as tutor, teaching all things (John 14:26). And the Holy Spirit is a believer's guide to truth throughout life (John 16:13).

The apostle Paul wrote more about the Holy Spirit in his 13 epistles than any other New Testament author. Refer to Romans 8, 1 Corinthians 2:12-14, 2 Corinthians 3, and Galatians 5 for more insight into the work of the Holy Spirit. In 1 Corinthians 2:1-5, Paul testifies to the Holy Spirit as his sole source of power to minister. He confessed that he was not an eloquent speaker or a wise teacher. In fact, Paul admitted that he was weak and fearful. He concluded that "my speech and my preaching were not with persuasive words of human wisdom, but in demonstration of the Spirit and of power, that your faith should not be in the wisdom of men but in the power of God" (1 Cor. 2:4-5). Is your power source found in men or in God? Do you depend on the power of God or your own human ability?

While God does give certain abilities to His creations, He wants to give them His power to do His work. As a leader, don't be limited to your own human abilities. Instead, unleash the power of the Holy Spirit as you lead. You will be able to accomplish so much more in His power than you could ever accomplish on your own. Your leadership skills will be strengthened as you depend on the power of the Holy Spirit.

I am grateful for the work of the Holy Spirit in my life. While God did give me some natural abilities, He has empowered me to lead beyond my own limits. As I speak to Christian women, the Holy Spirit gives me the words to connect the listeners to the heart of God. As I write Bible studies, the Holy Spirit fills my mind with insights to stimulate a passion for His Word. And as I teach, the Holy Spirit instructs me so that I can teach others. My source of power is obviously the Holy Spirit because I could never think those thoughts or speak those words. The Holy Spirit works through me when I am willing to accomplish His will. The Holy Spirit has definitely empowered me as I lead the women's ministry program at our seminary. God's will was much bigger than my dreams, but I obediently followed. Now the Lord has blessed abundantly as hundreds of women called to minister to other women are training to minister more effectively. How grateful I am for the power of the Holy Spirit working through me!

Now that you have been warned about the abuse of power and you have been reminded of the source of power, let's discuss the use of power. In what practical ways should leaders use their power for the good of others and to glorify God? **List below five ways leaders should use their power.**

THE USE OF POWER

Though some leaders abuse their power and other Christian leaders fail to depend on the power of the Holy Spirit, many effective leaders use their power in positive and productive ways. Let me suggest a few ways for power to be used for good and for God.

First, a leader can use her power **to accomplish God's will**. While the Holy Spirit is the original source of power, God can work through a leader and her position of responsibility to fulfill His will. Queen Esther is a perfect example of a leader whose position was used to accomplish God's will—to preserve the Jewish people. Today, God places Christian women in positions of leadership so they can be His vessels to accomplish His purpose.

Second, leaders can also use their power **to help others fulfill their dreams**. A visionary leader appreciates the vision of others and encourages them to pursue their dreams. My husband and I have a friend who aspires to accomplish some personal goals. It has been a joy to watch him accomplish his goals as my husband has supported him. By placing him in positions of leadership, my husband has helped him develop his gifts and fulfill his dreams. In many ways, Paul did that for young Timothy. As a spiritual leader, he gave his young friend and co-laborer opportunities to fulfill his God-given calling.

Third, leaders can use their power **to involve others in pursuing a vision**. An effective leader motivates others to join in the work. Jesus modeled for us the positive way that leaders can involve others. While He did not coerce the disciples to follow Him, Jesus did explain passionately why they should follow Him. As the power of the Holy Spirit drew them to Him, the twelve disciples became an important part of Jesus' ministry team. When a new leader begins her work, she must clearly communicate her vision and encourage others to follow her.

A fourth way that a leader can use her power is **to bring glory to God**. As God works through a leader she should focus attention on the Lord. People become vividly aware of God's power when great things are accomplished. The story of Miriam in the Old Testament is a clear example of a leader who glorified God in her accomplishments. Her song of praise said it this way: "Sing to the Lord, for He has triumphed gloriously!" (Exodus 15:21). Though an outstanding leader, Miriam redirected all praise to the Lord.

Fifth, a leader can use her power **to influence others to Jesus**. What a precious privilege to be able to bring someone to salvation because they look up to you as a leader! When God changes the life of a leader, her position can often lead others to a personal relationship with the Lord. The dramatic conversion of Lydia, a successful businesswoman, was used to bring her entire household to faith in Christ (Acts 16:11-15). Because of her position and her changed life, Lydia was able to make an eternal difference in the lives of those she led. That is another example of the positive use of power.

As we conclude, let's again consider what is power. James MacGregor Burns explains it this way in his book *Leadership*. "What is power? The 'power of A over B,' we are told, 'is equal to the maximum force which A can induce on B minus the maximum resisting force which B can mobilize in any direction.'" Think of this from the Christian perspective. If A is the Holy Spirit and B is the Christian leader, you can begin to understand the unlimited power of the Holy Spirit to strengthen the leader. As long as the leader is not resisting God's power or leaning too heavily on her own, the Holy Spirit can work through her in mighty ways. It is when we resist Him or seek our own wills that the power is limited. The Holy Spirit can mobilize the Christian leader to accomplish anything if she always remembers her source of power.

A LEADER'S LIFE

You may have some misgivings about the power you have as a leader. Use this time to evaluate how a leader's power can be used positively. Answer these questions honestly. How have you used your power for the good of others?

How have you used your power to glorify God?

Now thank God for the position of power He has given you. Then ask Him to keep you focused on your true source of power—the Holy Spirit.

"When leaders lead in Israel, when the people willingly offer themselves, bless the Lord!"
—Judges 5:2

A LEADER'S
LIGHT

A leader's style refers to her personal manner, unique behavior, or approach to leadership. Each leader has a style that becomes her own. Her style is a blend of her character, her experiences, and her skills. No one leadership style can be considered "most effective." In fact, it is essential for a leader to identify her own style, develop her skills, and not try to copy one another. Compromise of personal style is costly. The leader is discontent when not being true to herself and her work will be ineffective.

Personality styles have been studied for thousands of years. Hippocrates, the Greek physician and philosopher, identified specific personality differences in 400 BC. And in recent years much has been written about the personality types. In the Christian realm, well-known authors including Tim LaHaye, Florence Littauer, and Gary Smalley, have applied the knowledge of personalities or temperaments to human relationships and ministry. It is interesting to identify your own personality type and helpful to understand the personality types of others. **Why do you think an understanding of personalities is helpful to a leader?**

What do you think are the basic types of personalities?

I learned early in my ministry that I would be working with many different types of personalities. That was an important leadership lesson. The strengths and weaknesses of each personality are easily noted. And there is a need to balance groups, especially leadership teams, with different personalities. While some people may be easier to get along with, all personalities as well as all gifts are needed to minister to the whole body of Christ. One semester I taught a class for student wives at the seminary on "Personalities in Ministry." When my husband learned about this class, he said: "That's great. These ministers' wives will certainly meet some interesting personalities in the ministry." How true! While working with different personality types is often challenging, these differences are also a blessing.

In this lesson, we will study about a leader's style. We will begin with a review of the basic personality types and continue by examining several leadership styles. The lesson will conclude with a survey of biblical styles. It is helpful for a Christian leader to understand her own style, the styles of her leadership team, and the styles of those she works with in ministry.

PERSONALITY STYLES

There is no more interesting study than that of the personalities. It doesn't take long to realize that people are different. God truly demonstrates His sense of humor in creating so many people. And every personality has both strengths and weaknesses. When a leader's strengths get out of control, they become her weaknesses. As a Christian, you must work to improve your strengths and control your weaknesses. As a leader, the price is even higher because your weaknesses affect everyone else.

Hippocrates introduced the four basic temperaments. The *sanguine* is the magnetic personality (popular). The *choleric* is the commanding personality (powerful). The *melancholy* is the analytical personality (perfect). And the *phlegmatic* is the low-key personality (peaceful). Most people are a blend of the personalities though there is usually a dominant style. While there are numerous other classification systems, these four types are generally accepted.

Have you ever taken a personality inventory? Several characteristics of the four basic personality types are listed on the next page. Check the ones that apply to you and see if you can determine your predominant personality (adapted from *Personality Plus* by Florence Littauer).

Sanguine (Popular)

___ Magnetic personality
___ Talker with a sense of humor
___ Storyteller
___ Entertaining
___ Charming
___ Optimistic
___ Enthusiastic
___ Friendly
___ Cheerful
___ Creative and colorful

Melancholy (Perfect)

___ Analytical personality
___ Sensitive to others
___ Philosophical
___ Artistic and musical
___ Organizes on paper
___ Long-range goals
___ Schedule-oriented
___ Sees problems
___ Likes charts and graphs
___ Serious

Choleric (Powerful)

___ Commanding personality
___ Born leader
___ Goal-oriented
___ Logical thinker
___ Quick organizer
___ Takes control
___ Dynamic
___ Stimulates activity
___ Motivational
___ Confident

Phlegmatic (Peaceful)

___ Low-key personality
___ Cooperative
___ Diplomatic
___ Dry sense of humor
___ Well-balanced
___ Agreeable and pleasant
___ Steady and easygoing
___ Team-oriented
___ Good listener
___ Mediator

What is your primary personality type?

What are your strengths?

What are your weaknesses?

Leaders often seem to have powerful personalities because of their positions of leadership. But every leader has inborn personality traits. As a leader learns and grows, she can develop qualities from each personality type to help her become a better leader. In her intriguing book, *Put Power in Your Personality*, Florence Littauer examines the personalities of the US presidents. How interesting to see the differences. It is interesting to note that rarely do presidents with the same personality type succeed each other. And the most common personality type among the presidents is the Popular/Powerful combination. Beginning with the early twentieth century, see if you agree with the personalities Littauer identified for each president.

Franklin D. Roosevelt (1933-1945)	Popular/Powerful
Harry S. Truman (1945-1953)	Powerful
Dwight Eisenhower (1953-1961)	Peaceful
John F. Kennedy (1961-1963)	Popular/Powerful
Lyndon Johnson (1963-1969)	Powerful/Popular
Richard Nixon (1969-1974)	Perfect/Powerful
Gerald Ford (1974-1977)	Peaceful
Jimmy Carter (1977-1981)	Perfect
Ronald Reagan (1981-1989)	Popular
George Bush (1989-1993)	Peaceful
Bill Clinton (1993-2001)	Popular/Powerful
George W. Bush (2001-?)	(Littauer has not classified his personality type yet, but I would suggest Peaceful/Perfect)

It is important to understand that each person is born with a basic personality type. These inborn patterns added to life experiences prepare a person for leadership. To be an effective leader, an individual must overcome her weaknesses with her strengths. Leaders may be different in their appearances, backgrounds, and moral values, but their personality types will contribute to a similar style of leadership. The challenge for leaders is to "accentuate the positive, and eliminate the negative." Understanding your own personality style will help you as a leader.

There are as many different leadership styles as there are leaders. No two leaders are exactly alike. God has created each of us in His image but with a unique combination of features. Therefore leaders and their styles differ. And there is no one perfect style of leadership. Several basic leadership styles can be used to characterize leaders. Most leaders embody a combination of these leadership styles. It is helpful to understand these styles generally and to identify your own style specifically. Let's consider a few models of leadership styles.

Bob Dale presented four leadership styles in his book *Pastoral Leadership* (p. 40). When describing pastor-leaders he concluded that each fits into one of the following categories:

1. the **catalyst** leader
2. the **commander** leader
3. the **hermit** leader
4. the **encourager** leader

Each style of leadership has strengths and weaknesses. While the catalyst leader is a great team builder, she can develop a feeling of insignificance. While a commander leader inspires action, she can be too autocratic or authoritative. While a hermit leader is wise, she can seem to be aloof or disconnected. And while an encourager is a trusted counselor and friend, she may have poor management skills. It is important to recognize your leadership style then maximize your strengths and minimize your weaknesses.

Ken Blanchard introduced another helpful system of leadership styles in his book, *The One Minute Manager* (p. 30). He also suggested four leadership styles but his approach is from a different perspective. Consider the following leadership styles, which are descriptive of a leader's relationship to her followers.

1. **Directing**—the leader provides specific instructions and closely supervises task accomplishment.
2. **Coaching**—the leader continues to direct and closely supervises task accomplishment, but also explains decisions, solicits suggestions, and supports progress.
3. **Supporting**—the leader facilitates and supports subordinates' efforts toward task accomplishment and shares responsibility for decision-making with them.

4. **Delegating**—the leader turns over responsibility for decision-making and problem-solving to subordinates.

While there are settings where one type of leadership is more effective than another, there is no one style of leadership that is always perfect. A leader's challenge is to match the best style of leadership with the situation.

Now that we have considered two different descriptions of leadership styles, it is time for some self-evaluation. Can you identify your own style of leadership? **Using one of the systems presented previously, decide on your leadership type then discuss why.**

Is there a leadership style you desire to develop?

Why?

I have tried to honestly evaluate my own leadership style. Blanchard's models of leadership are helpful in describing my personal leadership style. Early in my ministry and even initially as a supervisor in my career, I was a director. I tended to give specific instructions and oversee closely. I took a more "hands-on" approach to leadership. There are still times when I direct—with new employees, new programs, or new ventures. However, I now find myself depending more on delegation, maybe because of increased responsibilities or limited time. But I also find it most effective to delegate. Those I work with seem to thrive as I turn responsibility over to them. And team spirit is promoted as we make decisions jointly and solve problems together. God has helped me develop the style of leadership most appropriate for the ministry He has called me to fulfill.

It is helpful for a leader to understand personality differences. But it is more important for a Christian leader to recognize biblical styles of leadership. The Lord can help you become a godly leader as you better understand yourself and your styles.

BIBLICAL STYLES

There are many outstanding leaders mentioned in the Bible. Men and women throughout Scripture led the people of God to accomplish His will. Each biblical leader had a unique personality and a unique leadership style. While we could consider many different leaders, let's focus on one outstanding female leader in the Bible. Take the time to read her story and learn from her leadership style.

Deborah, a prophetess, became a judge in Israel during the reign of the wicked King Jabin (Judges 4:3-4). She was a just judge who righteously led her people. Read her story in Judges chapters four and five. **After reading this passage, identify some characteristics of Deborah as a leader.**

In a time of oppression for the children of God, Deborah was recognized as a godly leader. During her service as judge, she led with authority from God (Judg. 4:4). She trusted God as she performed her work (Judg. 4:6). While she did her job, she delegated many tasks (Judg. 4:6-7). Deborah was a respected leader who motivated the people to follow her (Judg. 4:8-9). She served with a servant's heart (Judg. 4:9). And Deborah spoke with confidence of God's plan (Judg. 4:14). When God subdued the evil King Jabin and strengthened the Israelites, Deborah led a song of praise: "When leaders lead in Israel, when the people willingly offer themselves, bless the Lord!" (Judg. 5:2). You will be blessed as you take time to read the song of Deborah in Judges 5. It is an example of how godly leaders can celebrate the work of God in their lives.

Do you know someone who has assumed a leadership assignment from the Lord in a time of uncertainty? Even today, Christian leaders step out in faith and accept challenging positions if God directs them. We have a friend who was called by God to lead a Christian college as president. He left a position of security and entered a setting of uncertainty because he was confident of God's leadership. Many colleagues warned him of the risks, but he felt the power of God to lead the school in a positive direction. As he has trusted God and led with clear direction, God has blessed his tenure. The school has overcome its greatest obstacles and is again flourishing. God can work through the lives of godly leaders like Deborah and many others.

As you consider your own style as a leader, it is helpful to thank God for who He created you to be. He has given you the potential and the personality to lead effectively. He will also empower you to lead. Know who you are in Christ and who you are as a leader. Then evaluate your personality type and leadership style. Identify your own strengths and weaknesses. With the help of God and the encouragement of others, you can be a godly leader. Take time to study the individual styles of leaders in the Bible. Then make a lifelong commitment to lead only under the inspiration of the Holy Spirit.

A LEADER'S LIFE

In this lesson, you examined the leadership style of Deborah in the Bible. Are you like Deborah as a leader? Explain your answer.

Now pray the prayer of Deborah. "When leaders lead in Israel, when the people willingly offer themselves, bless the Lord!" (Judg. 5:2).

"But I discipline my body and bring it into subjection, lest, when I have preached to others, I myself should become disqualified."
—1 Corinthians 9:27

A LEADER'S LIGHT

Every leader must recognize her own limitations because even the strongest leaders can't do everything. Though we serve an awesome God, Christian leaders are human, with limitations, weaknesses, and failures. It is that basic understanding that focuses the glory on God when success is experienced in leadership. God can work powerfully through even an inadequate leader who fully trusts in the Lord.

John Maxwell has devoted his ministry to training Christian leaders. In his seminars and through his writings, Maxwell teaches biblical principles of leadership. He has identified five personal limitations that a leader must accept before she can lead effectively. Decide if you agree with his conclusions.

I cannot lead people <u>beyond</u> my leadership skills
I cannot lead people <u>above</u> my level of trust.
I cannot lead people <u>past</u> my level of commitment.
I cannot lead people <u>around</u> my undisciplined lifestyle.
I cannot lead people <u>without</u> my willingness to serve.

These are some personal limitations of all leaders. **Try to summarize these statements by John Maxwell in your own words so you can be reminded of your need to depend on God.**

I realize that as a leader I am unable to lead others if I am not trained, trustworthy, committed, disciplined, and selfless. If you acknowledge your own limitations and fully depend on God, you can lead His people in His power.

Paul the apostle took his responsibilities as a minister very seriously. He recognized his personal limitations, and he trusted in God with his whole heart. He did not want his human weaknesses to hinder the growth of God's people. So he continually committed himself to the Lord, praying for God's strength to overcome his own weaknesses. He disciplined himself daily with the power of the Holy Spirit. In 1 Corinthians 9:27, Paul said: "I discipline my body and bring it into subjection, lest, when I have preached to others, I myself should become disqualified." A Christian leader today must practice spiritual disciplines to overcome personal limitations and not be disqualified for leadership.

In this lesson, we will examine some general limitations of leaders—their personal limitations, weaknesses, and failures. As you read the Scripture and consider these principles, allow the Holy Spirit to reveal to you your own personal limitations. In recognizing your weaknesses, you are taking the first step toward effective leadership. Total dependence on God and personal discipline of self will add to a Christian leader's success.

PERSONAL LIMITATIONS

The progress of some leaders is limited by their own abilities and skills. Natural abilities and educational training help a leader serve more effectively. Without proper preparation, progress will be limited. There are examples of those with personal limitations in the Bible and in the Christian world today. The limitations of these leaders can teach all leaders why preparation is essential for leadership.

During the first missionary journey, Paul and Barnabas preached in Cyprus and Galatia (Acts 13-14). They were accompanied by young John Mark, their assistant (Acts 13:5). However, John Mark did not remain with them for the duration of the journey. Though the exact details are uncertain, it seems that the young missionary had some personal limitations. He left them in Perga and returned alone to Jerusalem. Take a few minutes to read this account in Acts 12:25-13:13. **Why do you think John Mark left Paul and Barnabas during their missionary journey?**

Later, Paul and Barnabas quarreled about John Mark's inclusion in the second missionary journey (Acts 15:38-39). For whatever reason, Paul did not think John Mark was prepared for the work. In time, John Mark did grow spiritually and mature in ministry. He traveled with Barnabas to minister in Cyprus and later wrote the gospel of Mark to Gentile Christians. Paul later commended the young man for his ministry (Philemon 24; Colossians 4:10; 2 Timothy 4:11). So the Holy Spirit helped him overcome his personal limitations.

Do you know someone who has been placed in a position of leadership that exceeded his or her abilities? Sometimes people are promoted beyond the level of their competence. Though they succeeded initially, failure comes because of their personal limitations. That is a shame. Workers will usually be content when they are fulfilled in their work, but they are frustrated when they cannot succeed. **Write the name here of someone you know who was unable to fulfill his/her position of responsibility.**

How did this person's personal limitations hinder his/her leadership?

Now pray that the Holy Spirit will help him/her overcome personal limitations.

Throughout the years, my husband and I have known several friends who were placed in positions of responsibility beyond their abilities and then struggled in their ministries. One friend who performed well as an assistant youth minister was unable to lead effectively as the full-time senior youth minister. It seemed he was promoted beyond his abilities. Another friend was successful when pastoring a small church, but struggled in a larger church.

It is always a blessing to see the many men and women called to ministry who make the necessary sacrifices for seminary training. While God certainly can use anyone who is willing and obedient, He is able to use ministers who are trained in an even more effective way. Twice each year in our seminary graduation, my husband reminds the graduates that in school they have added more tools to their toolboxes—skills and abilities to better equip them for the ministry God has called them to.

What are some basic skills needed for leadership? List these skills below and consider how a leader is limited if she doesn't possess these skills.

While required skills vary depending upon the type of work, most leaders need some general skills in order to succeed. Good judgment, wisdom and knowledge, decision-making abilities, tact and diplomacy, clear communication, organizational skills, good interpersonal relationships, and personal integrity are essential ingredients for leadership. Without these basic qualities, a leader is limited and doomed to failure. Now that we have considered some personal limitations, let's examine personal weaknesses that would hinder successful leadership.

PERSONAL WEAKNESSES

Some leaders have personal limitations; their lack of skills and abilities hinders their leadership. Other leaders have personal weaknesses or flaws in their personal character. In the book, *Spiritual Leadership: Responding to God's Call*, J. Oswald Sanders identifies some weaknesses of leaders (pp. 127-133). He calls them perils of leadership. These personal weaknesses have certainly contributed to the failure of some leaders—pride, egotism, jealousy, popularity, infallibility, indispensability, and elation/depression. Let's briefly discuss each one.

• **Pride** or conceit puts self on the throne and God in the background. When a leader takes credit for her own gifts and abilities, she develops an attitude of pride. A proud person is disqualified from serving the Lord. **What does Proverbs 16:5 teach us about how God feels about pride?**

The Lord considers pride to be an abomination—He despises pride.

• **Egotism** is an exaggerated form of pride. When a leader praises herself or magnifies her own attainments, she is actually revealing her weaknesses. Egotism centers on self. **What does Proverbs 14:16 say about an egotistical person?**

One who is full of self or self-confident is a fool, is not wise.

• **Jealousy** is intolerance toward the success of others or an attitude of suspicion toward rivals. When a leader is jealous of another person, she is reflecting poor confidence in herself and her abilities. The Bible speaks of the perils of jealousy and the sin of covetousness, greed or envy. **What does Proverbs 14:30 say about envy or jealousy?**
The Bible says that a person who is jealous is rotten to the bones. Jealousy is a significant weakness for a Christian leader. Moses did not let jealousy

hinder his work. He asked Joshua, "Are you zealous for my sake?" (Num. 11:29). Then he declared, "Oh that all the Lord's people were prophets and that the Lord would put His Spirit upon them!" Moses did not let feelings of jealousy limit his leadership.

• **Popularity** is a subtle personal weakness in some leaders. While all leaders want to be liked, it is unhealthy for leaders to seek to be on a pedestal. Too many leaders have fallen from that pedestal because of their human frailties. Paul had to warn his followers about choosing one minister of the gospel over another. When some Christians favored Apollos and others favored Paul, he immediately warned them. **Read 1 Corinthians 3:5-7 and summarize his warning about popularity.**

The focus should always be on the Lord, not the leader. Today, Christian women must be careful not to favor one Bible teacher or writer or speaker over another. Remember that God is using them to draw people to Himself. Popularity among teenagers is problematic and it can be problematic when uncontrolled among Christian leaders.

• **Infallibility** is impossible in leadership because of human limitations. No one is perfect and all leaders will make mistakes. While a Spirit-filled leader will make fewer mistakes in judgment, even the most spiritually mature leader will err. It is defeating to suppose that a leader is perfect or incapable of error. The disciples often demonstrated this human tendency. When the disciples made wrong assumptions or false accusations, Jesus corrected them. Read the account of Jesus and the hemorrhaging woman in Luke 8:43-48. **How did He correct the disciples when they made mistakes?**

A leader's influence is increased when she willingly admits her mistakes and asks for forgiveness and help.
• **Indispensability** refers to a leader's false sense of significance, or unwillingness to give up authority to others. As a leader serves, she often becomes consumed with her work and convinced that her involvement is necessary. Christian leaders must gladly pass the mantle of leadership on to younger leaders. Otherwise, God's work may stagnate or His chosen may not be leading. At Saul's death, David became king.

Read his words of commissioning to David in 1 Samuel 24:16-22. How did Saul transition power to David?

Saul hesitantly relinquished his throne to David. He may have thought himself indispensable. But, David did become king. No leader is indispensable.

• Finally, **elation** and **depression** can be a personal weakness for a leader. If you have never been in a position of leadership, you may not understand this peril. In leadership, there are days of great joy and days of deep sorrow. There are extreme highs and lows, celebrations and disappointments. A leader is weakened if she overreacts to the victories or defeats. It is easy to be elated by successes and depressed by failures. Jesus tried to focus His disciples on the priority of the work so they wouldn't experience elation and depression in ministry. Read Luke 10:20 and decide how Jesus counseled the disciples to respond to their successes.

A leader should always focus on the eternal and not the temporal—spiritual rewards not earthly gains. A friend who recently went into full-time Christian ministry shared that the weekends were mountaintops and Mondays were valleys. She was overjoyed as she ministered but let down when returning home. A leader in women's ministry can experience the "highs" during a dynamic special event and the "lows" when it is over. Leaders must beware of elation/depression and these other perils of leadership.

PERSONAL FAILURES

In addition to personal limitations and personal weaknesses, some leaders also experience personal failures. When mistakes are made, a leader's failures are publicly exposed. While no one likes to fail, failure is inevitable. And the more risks involved in your work, the greater the likelihood of failures. Christian leaders must understand their personal failures are human, accept the forgiveness of God and others, and continue on.

I tend to be a perfectionist. Yes, I am a self-confessed obsessive-compulsive. I like everything to be just right. I don't like to admit I am wrong, and I definitely don't like to make mistakes. Can you identify? I read a helpful quote years ago that encourages me when I have blown it. "Lapses are the rule not the exception" (Cooper, p. 79). While Ken Cooper, "father of aerobics," said that about exercise, I believe it applies to all areas of life—even leadership. It is much more common for people to fail than for people not to fail. That truth should help you handle your own failures.

Christians in very visible positions of leadership throughout the years have failed because of human weaknesses and personal sin. Their failures hurt the leaders themselves as well as their families and the cause of Christ.

The failures may be moral, financial, physical, emotional, or spiritual. I had personal experience with moral failure when my evangelist father left the Lord, the ministry, and our family due to sin in his life. Even though he has been forgiven and our relationship has been restored, my dad continues to experience the consequences of sin.

Personal failure also includes making mistakes. When a leader makes a wrong choice, the work and the people suffer along with the leader herself. The mistakes of a leader are public embarrassments. A leader is also hurt by the failures of others. When a leader entrusts responsibility to a co-worker and the co-worker fails to complete her assignment or makes an error in judgment, the leader is greatly disappointed. Some leaders have been hurt by the failures of their children. Billy and Ruth Graham were heartbroken when their son, Franklin, rebelled, but they trusted God and continued in their calling. In time, Franklin Graham returned to the Lord and is now serving with his father in ministry. The Grahams had faith that their prodigal child would someday return and that personal failure didn't hinder their ministry.

The Bible records two accounts of fathers who had faith and continued to serve the Lord even when their children were disobedient. Read a portion of the story about Eli and his sons in 1 Samuel 2:22-25. How did Eli the priest, respond to the personal failures of his children?

Eli rebuked his sons for their sins against God, but their behavior didn't change. Their personal failures led to separation from God and their godly father. Eli learned of the deaths of his sons, Hophni and Phinehas, before his own death (1 Sam. 4:17). The prodigal children died in their sin, but the faithful priest Eli was able to train young Samuel to be a great prophet and priest in Israel.

Samuel himself suffered because of the personal failures of his own children. Born in fulfillment of barren Hannah's prayers and trained by Eli in the Shiloh sanctuary (1 Sam. 2:11), Samuel prophesied, judged, and led the people according to God's will. **Read a portion of Samuel's story in 1 Samuel 8. How did Samuel respond to the personal failures of his children?**

Heartbroken by the rebellion of his sons whom he had made judges, Samuel warned them and the elders of Israel about God's penalty for disobedience. But the sins of his children didn't hinder the effective leadership of Samuel. He trusted God to lead through him and to deal with his children. These two biblical accounts are clear examples of how leaders today should continue to do God's will even in the face of personal failures. However, some types of personal failure do disqualify a leader from ministry.

In this lesson, several limitations in leadership have been identified, biblical examples have been cited, and current illustrations have been discussed. In closing, you must be reminded of your own personal limitations as a leader. If Paul the apostle was constantly aware of his weaknesses and totally dependent on God, Christian leaders today should follow his example. Because of his devotion and discipline, God blessed his ministry greatly. He led many people to Jesus, started dozens of churches, and wrote half of the New Testament. In 1 Corinthians 9:27, Paul said: "But I discipline my body and bring it into subjection, lest, when I have preached to others, I myself should become disqualified." He is a role model of godly leadership and the Scripture is a clear command to trust God to overcome your weaknesses with God's supernatural strength.

A LEADER'S LIFE

Can you think of other personal limitations a leader may possess? There was only time in this lesson to briefly discuss a few. List any additional limitations below under the column labeled "what" then describe how that weakness limits the leader's leadership.

What?

How?

Now pray that God will overcome your weaknesses with His strength.

"I have learned in whatever state I am, to be content. . . I can do all things through Christ who strengthens me."—Philippians 4:11, 13

A LEADER'S LIGHT

In the previous lesson, you considered the limitations, personal weaknesses, and failures which are experienced by all leaders. Before continuing the discussion of a leader's challenges—those placed on her by difficult people, difficult circumstances, and difficult work—I wanted to share with you a recipe. A friend of mine, Becky Brown, recently wrote a recipe for "Cake of the Weak" (yes, it is "weak" not "week"). Her ingredients and instructions are a profound reminder of a leader's personal limitations. As you read this recipe, ask God to help you remain strong.

Cake of the Weak

Recipe: One cup of marching with hidden sin. One cup of leading without direction from the Lord. A pinch of pride. A dash of fear. Mix with defiance and prayerlessness. Bake until burnt. The cookbook index title of this cake is "Double Decker Failure Deluxe." It plays to rave reviews such as: "This cake has fallen and it can't get up!"

Suggested toppings: Confrontation and Reprimand.

Recommended side dishes: Repentance and Confession.

WARNING: The Great Physician has declared that production and/or consumption of this cake could be hazardous to your spiritual health. It could potentially paralyze your spiritual walk. It could contribute to cloudiness of your spiritual vision. Partake with fear and trembling or preferably not at all.

Yes, all leaders have personal limitations but they also face leadership challenges. There are people, circumstances, and tasks beyond their control. These challenges often hinder the success of a leader. Goals cannot be accomplished and progress cannot be made when leaders face distracting challenges. In the last lesson, you learned about some obstacles faced by leaders. You considered five personal limitations suggested by John Maxwell. He also suggested several other leadership challenges. He called them "people limitations." Read his conclusions below.

~ *I cannot lead people* longer *than they're willing to follow.*

~ *I cannot lead people* farther *than they're willing to go.*

~ *I cannot lead people* faster *than they're willing to charge*

~ *I cannot lead people* higher *than they're willing to climb.*

All leaders must accept *personal* limitations and *people* limitations if they truly desire to lead effectively.

Many variables contribute to these leadership challenges. The people, setting, or tasks can make a leader's work difficult. In addition, the culture and the context contribute to potential leadership challenges. While the circumstances may be different, one thing is certain—all leaders will face leadership challenges. While the circumstances may be difficult, one thing is certain—all leaders will face leadership challenges. These challenges are experienced even among church leaders. Challenges are inevitable.

What are some of the most common challenges you have faced in leadership? (Be sure to include difficult people, tough circumstances, and hard work.)

I am grateful that I learned to handle work challenges early in my professional career. As a speech pathologist working in a medical setting, I found myself working among a group of negative people, in a stressful situation, doing difficult work. That challenging environment took a toll on me not only because I was inexperienced, but because I was naive about people and their personalities. I learned that I could become like them if I didn't trust God for strength and persevere in a godly life. God taught me how to handle challenges as He taught me patience, perseverance, and love. It is essential for leaders to learn how to deal with inevitable challenges and become effective leaders.

DIFFICULT PEOPLE

While people are one of the greatest blessings of leadership, people can also be one of the greatest challenges. People can bring tremendous joy and people can also cause tremendous heartbreak. A leader must understand how to work with difficult people. A leader must learn to forgive people who disappoint. And a Christian leader must know how to depend on God even when people are impossible to work with.

In his book, *The Empowered Leader*, Calvin Miller suggested that there are several types of difficult souls(pp. 140-153). If you have not already met these difficult people in your position of leadership, you will. They are in every church, every office, and on every committee.

1. The *Chronically Arrogant*—People who have strong opinions and harsh personalities. They are often pushy and controlling.

2. The *Congenitally Belligerent*—People who have been "upset since the womb." They are always angry, negative, and critical.

3. The *Non-Negotiator*—People who may remain silent but undermine the leadership. They often complain and manipulate.

4. The *Nit-Picker*—People who major on the minors. They focus on small irrelevant details, which distract from the leader's vision.

5. The *Wheedler*—A word that combines whining and needling, these people complain and groan about everything. They whine continually and irritate everyone.

6. The *"Yes-Butter"*—People who seem to agree yet always have a negative comment. They are nay-sayers who try to prejudice the feelings of others.

A leader must recognize these difficult people and overcome their challenges. A leader must know her challengers then seek to work with them constructively. **Have you encountered some difficult people in your leadership? How did these difficult souls impact your ability to lead? Briefly describe your response to them.**

In every church, there are some challenging people. I have met my share. And I have learned much by watching other leaders deal with them in a godly way. At a time of transition in my own church, these difficult people seemed to surface in an effort to undermine the leadership of our pastor. At an especially tense business meeting, I took Calvin Miller's book to church with me. During the heated discussion, I tried to identify the "difficult souls." It helped me to see the critical man as chronically arrogant and the caustic woman as congenitally belligerent. I quickly identified one lady as a nitpicker when she asked a dozen questions about very small details. I had to refrain from laughing when one man said "yes-but" about three times in his comments. In that two-hour church business meeting, I learned so much about difficult people that will benefit my ministry. Though at times their comments were inappropriate, they were handled with courtesy and concern. I learned a valuable lesson—to love difficult people and pray for them.

Christian leaders in the Bible were challenged by difficult people, and the early church had difficult members. Do you remember the New Testament story of two women who were fighting? What a challenge for Paul and the church leaders to deal with these ladies in a godly way. Read the account in Philippians 4:2-7. **What did Paul say about these difficult ladies?**

Though we don't know exactly what their conflict was about, the Bible clearly reveals that the ladies were troubled. They were causing unrest in the church and opposing the leadership. They may have had personality differences. They may have been jealous of each other. Or they may have had different opinions about important issues. Whatever their differences, their conflict was challenging to the church leadership.

Paul advised those ladies how to reconcile their differences. He gave us a model for resolving conflict and coping with problem people. He preached a sermon about humility and unity. That lesson will help Christian leaders today face leadership challenges. In Philippians 3:15-16, Paul said: "Therefore let us, as many as are mature, have this mind; and if in anything you think otherwise, God will reveal even this to you. Nevertheless, to the degree that we have already attained, let us walk by the same rule, let us be of the same mind."

DIFFICULT CIRCUMSTANCES

Christian leaders today will inevitably meet difficult people, and they will also face difficult circumstances. No matter how gifted or godly the leader, there are some challenging life situations. Some leaders are unable to overcome these obstacles. Other leaders face these obstacles and with the help of the Lord succeed in their leadership. God wants you to trust Him to see you through these difficult circumstances and create among His people the "same mind."

There was a godly woman in the Old Testament times who lived in challenging circumstances but was used by God in a mighty way. Read about Abigail in 1 Samuel 25:2-3. **How did Abigail face her difficult circumstances?**

What can you learn from Abigail that will help you as a leader?

Abigail was married to a wicked man. The Bible says it this way: "the man was harsh and evil in his doings" (1 Sam. 25:3). He was an abusive husband. But Abigail didn't let her difficult circumstances hinder her leadership. Even in a bad marriage, God used her to lead her household. Abigail protected them by wisely going to King David with a warning. God honored her faithfulness even in her tough situation (1 Sam. 25:23-35). After her husband's death, Abigail married King David and became a part of the royal household.

Christian leaders today may face marital problems like Abigail. Or they may experience staff conflict, time limitations, or hostile environments. Each obstacle is major, but no obstacle is too great for God. Prayer is essential for a godly resolution of such leadership challenges. And God can be glorified even amidst trying experiences.

A growing area of ministry is church planting. Ministers are called to begin Christian work in pioneer areas, parts of the country where there is little organized religion. These faithful servants often face insurmountable obstacles. Far from home, in remote areas, without peer support, there is little support or encouragement. We have friends who were called to start churches in a remote area, resistant to religion, and in very cold weather. How challenging to do the work of the Lord in such harsh conditions! How difficult to raise young children far from family! But in very real ways, God affirmed the call and provided for the needs. God has used this precious family even in their toughest times to bring hope to others.

DIFFICULT WORK

Christian leaders often face the challenge of difficult people. Others face the challenge of difficult circumstances. Some face the challenge of difficult work. There are some leaders who will face all of these challenges in the course of their ministries. But remember, no challenge is too great for God. A leader must learn to trust in Him and not believe the criticism of others. A leader must find rest in the Lord and not be stressed by work. And a leader must seek renewal of passion and not burn out from discouragement. Let's discuss each of these leadership challenges that result from difficult work.

Every leader will receive **criticism** from others. In fact, a leader who is not criticized by someone is probably not leading. People will always have opposing opinions or negative feedback. A Christian leader must learn from criticism but not take it personally. One sign of mature leadership is healthy response to criticism. Leaders should learn these ways of receiving negative criticism:

1. Seek God's confirmation of the criticism.
2. Don't become defensive.
3. Listen completely and carefully.
4. Ask for evidence or examples.

5. Clarify the real problem.
6. Be aware of personal blind spots or weaknesses.
7. Determine the motive of the critic.
8. Discuss the criticism with God and a wise counselor.
9. Decide the appropriate action.
10. Learn from the criticism, then leave the matter to God.

God has been teaching me how to accept personal criticism. I don't like it, and I often don't understand it, but I try to learn from it. It is much harder for me to accept criticism by others of my husband's leadership. Because I love him so much and I believe in his vision wholeheartedly, I take criticism of him very personally. I have to pray for love and patience when I hear someone question his vision. I have to seek forgiveness and understanding when someone tries to undermine his work. I often turn to a trusted friend for encouragement and counsel when others cast doubt. It has been difficult, but I am learning how to handle the inevitable criticism of others. After all, they are sinful souls like I am.

Stress and burnout are common complaints of leaders. The many demands of life pull a leader in different directions. Frequent crises and unresolved conflict can add to the pressure of an already demanding life. In fact, burnout in ministry is becoming epidemic in proportion. Many leaders in the church are becoming mentally, physically, and spiritually exhausted. Difficult people, difficult circumstances, and difficult work add to the stress. As a result, ministries are failing and ministers are faltering. Christian leaders must learn to recognize stress and cope with it to prevent burnout and failure. With the help of the Lord, you can overcome the greatest obstacles, and you can survive the toughest circumstances. In fact, healthy management of stress can actually produce positive results and prevent future burnout.

If you are under stress and facing burnout, you must turn to the Lord in fervent prayer. God will ease your burden and lift your load (Matt. 11:28-30). You may need to back away from some of your duties and ease your workload. It may help for you to delegate some of your responsibilities to others. But most importantly, you must learn to relax and take time for yourself. In the quiet moments of life, God can rebuild and restore. But a weary leader must let go of the work and let God have His way.

If any person in the Bible had good reason to be stressed, it was the woman of Proverbs 31. She had so much to do. While she was a godly woman who feared the Lord, she was also hardworking. At the end of her long days, she must have been tired. When juggling her responsibilities, she must have been frustrated. As daily crises arose, she must have been stressed. But this virtuous woman always trusted God and always lived out her faith.

Read Proverbs 31:10-31 and identify some of the work done by this industrious woman. **Write her job description below.**
The Proverbs 31 woman was a _____

Now fill in blanks below from the Scripture to explain how she managed her difficult work.
verse 17—she _____ herself
verse 20—she _____ others
verse 30—she _____ the Lord

The Proverbs 31 woman was able to reduce stress and prevent burnout because she strengthened herself, served others, and sought the Lord. What a wonderful example for busy women!

How should a leader handle inevitable challenges? In the book *Transformed Lives*, Chris Adams suggested a biblical response to conflict (pp. 176-177). These nine steps can also help a leader know how to react to external challenges.

1. Do nothing. Take a break from the people and situation. Distance from the challenge can give a fresh perspective.

2. Exhibit self-control. Respond slowly and do not over-react. Impulsive responses often lead to regret.

3. Stop, think—and pray. As you pause and reflect, be sure to pray. Ask for God's guidance.

4. Ask yourself, is the issue worth pressing? The challenge may be insignificant. If so, forget it and move on. If not, continue the process of resolution.

5. Evaluate your own attitudes, strengths, and weaknesses. Try to determine your role in the challenges. Ask God to identify your successes and failures.

6. Follow scriptural guidelines. God's Word gives directions for facing any conflict and all challenges. (See Matthew 18:15-16, Rom. 12:17-21, and James 1:19-20.)

7. Ask questions for clarification. Gather accurate information and handle any miscommunication.

8. Discover those things on which you do agree. In other words, try to focus on the positive. Find points of agreement and mutual benefit.

9. Take some time apart. Wait on the Lord to work in your own life, the lives of others, and the situation.

The apostle Paul gave advice to Christians who were facing challenges. His advice still applies today. In Philippians 4:11-13 he said: "I have learned in whatever state I am, to be content. I know how to be abased, and I know how to abound. Everywhere and in all things I have learned both to be full and to be hungry, both to abound and to suffer need. I can do all things through Christ who strengthens me." Paul learned to be content when facing criticism or receiving praise. He was joyful in difficult circumstances or abundant blessings. His example can teach leaders today how to face challenges—challenges from difficult people, difficult work, and difficult circumstances.

A Leader's Life

Every Christian leader faces challenges with difficult people, in tough circumstances, and from hard work. Take a few moments to remember some challenging leadership situations you have faced. Then remember God's response to your challenges. Record your answers in the spaces below.

My Situation

God's Solution

Aren't you grateful that God has the solution to every leadership challenge? Thank Him for His supernatural solutions.

"And He called the twelve to Himself, and began to send them out two by two, and gave them power over unclean spirits."—Mark 6:7

A LEADER'S LIGHT

Until this point in the Bible study, the focus has been on the leader: *you.* We have discussed a leader's work, calling, and vision. We have examined a leader's lifestyle, power, and style. And we have honestly identified a leader's limitations and challenges. In this lesson, we will move our focus to those we work with in leadership: *the team.* The work that God has called us to do will be done more effectively and with greater ease as we work together with others called to lead.

Jesus illustrated the importance of teamwork in His own ministry. As He began His work on earth, Jesus Christ the Savior of the world called disciples to follow alongside Him, not because He was unable to do the work alone but because God desires to work through many. The example of Jesus calling, equipping, and sending His disciples helps leaders today understand the importance of working with a team and training them for ministry. This lesson will explore a leader's team—how to find team members, train them, and multiply them.

Before we begin the specific study, take a few minutes to read the accounts of Jesus appointing His disciples in three of the four gospels—Matthew 10:4; Mark 3:13-19; Luke 6:12-16. (These are the Synoptic Gospels, which document the life and ministry of Jesus, while the Gospel of John explains the meaning of Jesus' ministry. The book of John does not include a record of Jesus appointing His disciples.) Now that you have read those passages, answer the following questions: **How did Jesus appoint His disciples?**

Why did Jesus choose 12 disciples?

Jesus began His ministry in Galilee by preaching repentance (Matt. 4:12-17; Mark 1:14-15; Luke 4:14-15). Immediately He called four fishermen to be His disciples—Peter, Andrew, James, and John (Matt. 4:18-22; Mark 1:16-20; Luke 5:1-11). Then He chose eight more men (Matt. 10:2-4; Mark 3:18-19; Luke 6:14-16). Together they ministered by preaching, teaching, and healing. As they served, Jesus trained His disciples (Matt. 10:1; Mark 3:13-15; Luke 6:12-13). And later He sent them out to minister in His name (Matt. 10:5-15; Mark 6:7-13; Luke 9:1-6). Jesus called 12 disciples to work directly with Him though He had many other apostles. He selected the 12, His ministry team, because of their willingness to follow Him, not because of their abilities. They had a variety of backgrounds, personalities, gifts, talents, and vocations. But they served the Lord together in order to accomplish one purpose: to spread the gospel message of salvation.

Who is your ministry team? Who are the people serving the Lord with you? Who are the people you are responsible for leading? Are you leading them to follow God's will? In your home, your ministry team is your family—your children. God has given you the responsibility of leading them to Him. In your church, your ministry team may be a Sunday School class or Bible study group. You are to lead them to a mature faith in Christ and deeper knowledge of His Word. In your work, you may lead your colleagues into a personal relationship with Jesus Christ by your Christlike example and words of truth. And in the community, you have the responsibility of leading others to Jesus as you minister to them in the name of the Lord. In each situation, you are more effective as a Christian leader if other Christians are working with you—a godly father, a faithful co-leader, a caring coworker, or a loving neighbor. God has given you a team to help accomplish His purpose. Now let's discuss how to find the team, train the team, and multiply the team.

FINDING THE TEAM

Where did Jesus look to find His disciples? The answer is simple but difficult. He looked everywhere. He found 12 men from different places and different vocations. He didn't just look in one town or one setting or one workplace. He didn't choose only people He knew or with backgrounds like His. Jesus called 12 men with unique gifts and diverse experiences to minister with Him. He launched a careful, prayerful search to find His ministry team. That's what you should do, too. In some situations, a leader is delegated to lead a particular group. But, in most circumstances, a leader has some input in selecting a ministry team. Let's consider some biblical principles and practical suggestions for selecting a leadership team.

Mark clearly recorded the first step of Jesus in choosing His disciples: "And He went up on the mountain and called to Him those He Himself wanted" (Mark 3:13). **What did Jesus most often do when He went up to the mountain?**

Read the following Scriptures to be reminded of Jesus' activity on the mountain: Matthew 14:23; Mark 1:35; Luke 22:39-42. When Jesus went to the mountain or to the wilderness or to a solitary place, He typically desired to be alone, to talk to His Father, and to seek God's will. Prayer is the first step in the team selection process. As you pray, you depend on God to help you find those He has called to serve. You also ask His Spirit to precede you in opening their hearts to accept the position of service.

There are other practical considerations in the selection of a leadership team. Talk with your pastor and other church staff members about suggestions for people to serve in positions of leadership. In addition, you may find out about volunteers through a survey of interests and gifts or from advertising the vacant positions in a church publication. You should also keep your eyes open, looking for candidates in unusual places. Move beyond your own church area and seek others who may be qualified to serve. Be aware of new members coming into the church and help them find a place of service. It may be wise to start small, seeking only one or two other workers until the work expands. Remember the model of Jesus who first chose four disciples and then added eight more as the ministry increased. You will be surprised as you pray and patiently wait that God will bring you the leadership team He has fashioned for His work.

It has been my personal experience as a leader in women's ministry at my own church that God has brought together a team of gifted ladies to do His work. While our women's ministry began as my burden for the women of our church, God has placed a similar call on the lives of 14 other women. After much prayer and consultation with our pastor, God has raised up a group of very different ladies with a passion for the Lord, a commitment to His church, and a concern for other women. We represent different ages and stages of life and come from varied backgrounds and professions, but we are united in the will of God. It is exciting to see God work through dedicated women—singles, seniors, wives, mothers, and professionals. He can do that through your leadership team if you pray fervently and seek His guidance in selecting those to serve that He has chosen.

Read Mark 2:13-14 to see how Jesus chose Matthew to be His disciple. **Now describe the selection process of Jesus.**

Jesus was again ministering to the multitudes. But as He was busy teaching and preaching, He still took time to notice Matthew, a tax collector. Jesus saw his need and noticed his potential. Then Jesus called to Matthew, "Follow Me," and Matthew did. As a leader, you will oftentimes be busy doing your work. Be sure to learn from Jesus. Never be too busy to notice the needs and potential of others. Volunteers may be all around you awaiting an opportunity to serve. You may have the privilege of extending to them the call from God, "Follow Me." And they may become significant contributors to your leadership team. Finding the team is a first challenge of leadership, training them is the next challenge.

TRAINING THE TEAM

In her book *Designing Effective Women's Ministries*, Jill Briscoe said, "Leadership development is an act of loving and leading your leaders" (p. 103). How true! Once you have identified your team members, you must train them. Just because they volunteered or you volunteered them (some churches elect leaders when they are not present to decline!), they are not necessarily prepared to do the work. The leaders in your team must be trained—their leadership skills must be developed. While training is challenging, a leader is blessed to see novices become experts in ministry as they develop skills and depend on the Holy Spirit for power. As a leader, your role is to love your team members as you lead them.

Once Jesus selected His twelve disciples, He trained them before sending them out to minister. In Mark 6:7-13, Jesus gave the disciples some very practical advice. He called them to Himself and gave them a list of dos and don'ts for the road. He said do take a staff and do wear sandals. Don't take a bag or bread or money. Then Jesus empowered them to minister and sent them out two by two. Jesus equipped those He had called before He sent them out. He taught them to depend on Him for their basic needs. Training in ministry is essential.

Paul also instructed young Timothy before sending him out to minister. **Read 1 Timothy 4:11-16; then list six different instructions given by Paul to Timothy.**

1.
2.
3.
4.
5.
6.

Paul equipped young Timothy in practical ways. He began by telling him to teach what Paul had outlined (v. 11). He told him to be an example in all that he said or did, even though some would criticize his youth and inexperience (v. 12). Paul continued by challenging Timothy to devote himself to the reading and teaching of Scripture (v. 13). And he encouraged Timothy to develop his spiritual gifts of teaching and preaching the gospel (v. 14). Paul taught Timothy to be diligent in his personal and spiritual disciplines (v. 15). And he concluded with a challenge to persevere in his faith and ministry (v. 16). What a clear training protocol! What solid biblical counsel about leadership development! These biblical lessons can help leaders today know how to train others for leadership.

Based on these Scriptures and others, let's summarize how to train your leadership team. As the search process began in prayer, so must the training process. So begin by praying that God will guide you, the leader, and that He will instruct them, the team. Then you will want to study the Bible to learn more about God's call and His work. There are many other excellent books about leadership as well as training conferences. Try to learn about leading, so you can share your knowledge with others. It will be important to clearly share the ministry vision and purpose with the team so they can adopt it and seek to accomplish it. Throughout the process of training, the leader must teach by working alongside the team members. Not only is that a model of servant leadership, but it is instruction by doing. Encouragement is essential during training because risks are involved and failures are inevitable. Constant monitoring, evaluation, and assistance must be provided as a part of leadership training. And be sure to recognize accomplishments and acknowledge effort. Your team will be strengthened by your positive affirmatives and constructive feedback.

Jill Briscoe summarized leadership training with five I's and I added one of my own. So consider these six action words that begin with the letter I and guide leaders in training others to serve. In training the leadership team, a leader should:

Involve—Include them in goal setting and decision-making.
Inspire—Challenge them to do the work of the Kingdom.
Instruct—Teach them what to do and how to do it.
Instill—Create in them a concern for ministry.
Intercede—Pray for your leaders without ceasing.
Interact—Work with your leaders as they learn to do God's will.

I am blessed by my fellow servants. God has surrounded me with precious Christians with whom to minister. I am grateful for a leadership team in women's ministry at our church that works to meet the needs of the women in our church and community. I am grateful for a support staff at the New Orleans Baptist Theological Seminary that enables me to lead student wives and women's ministry students. I am most grateful for a supportive husband who encourages me to use my spiritual gifts to serve the Lord. We are a team—a ministry team—devoted to Kingdom work. God has brought them into my life. He has called us to labor together, and now He is equipping us for service. As a leader, I am responsible for training those who work with me. But as a leader, I am also in need of growth and maturity. A leader who is growing personally and equipping others will be fruitful in ministry and multiply the team. Multiplication is God's plan.

MULTIPLYING THE TEAM

God chose to begin His work with a few and then multiply His work as they reached others, and Christian leaders today need to follow that example. Leaders have the privilege of influencing others and the responsibility of raising up the next generation of leaders. But multiplication in ministry doesn't just happen. Each leader must consciously multiply herself. There is no greater joy than seeing God touch the lives of others through your ministry and, in turn, work through them in positions of leadership.

Timothy was a follower of Christ and leader in the early church. His work for the Lord began small and then multiplied. The results of His ministry continue today through the spread of the church of Jesus Christ. Timothy, who was discipled by the apostle Paul, also discipled others to do the Lord's work. He visited the early churches in Thessalonica, Corinth, Philippi, and Ephesus. While there, Timothy helped the churches in many ways. He encouraged doctrinal stability and developed organizational systems. Before leaving each church, Timothy multiplied himself through local leaders.

Paul gave instruction to Timothy and others to pass on this legacy of godly leadership as faithful leaders. Read 2 Timothy 2:1-7. **What did Paul teach Timothy about multiplying leaders?**

Rewrite 2 Timothy 2:2 in your own words.

Paul outlined for Timothy a pattern of multiplication in ministry. In fact, this passage illustrates spiritual multiplication through four generations—Paul, Timothy, Timothy's followers, and their followers. Kingdom work would have been limited if the Lord chose to work only through Paul. But because Paul discipled many who then discipled others, the Kingdom work was multiplied.

Paul also gave specific instructions to women when in Titus 2:3-5. He said the older women should admonish the young women to love their husbands and children, to live godly lives, and to serve the Lord faithfully. As women influence other women for God, the ministry is multiplied. No one woman can do all the work of the Lord. Thus God empowers one to reach another as spiritual growth is multiplied.

With great gratitude, I reflect on the way God has multiplied His work through me—one woman committed to the Lord and passionate in my desire to draw women closer to Him. Through my spiritual mentor, JoAnn Leavell, I learned many ways to serve the Lord and lead effectively. Through my ministry God has reached many women who have been called to women's ministry. Now through the ministries of their own churches, those women are leading other women. As Paul noted in 2 Timothy 2:2, at least four generations of leaders have been used by God in my life. What a testimony of the spiritual multiplication of God! God builds His leadership team one member at a time. As one leader develops another leader, God's work will be multiplied.

In his book, *Jesus on Leadership: Becoming a Servant Leader*, Gene Wilkes identified a five-step plan for equipping others for ministry, using an acrostic for the word *EQUIP*.

Encourage them to serve (1 Thess. 5:11).

Qualify them for service (2 Tim. 2:2).

Understand their needs (Luke 11:1).

Instruct them (1 Tim. 4:11).

Pray for them as they serve (John 17:6-19).

This is a simple but significant process for leadership training. It is a biblical plan for equipping the saints. It can also be used to evaluate the effectiveness of a leader. As a leader, are you equipping those who serve with you? Are you preparing others to lead? While leadership is a precious privilege, it also bears heavy responsibilities—the responsibility to train those who serve with you.

As you consider your responsibility to develop other leaders, thank God for the spiritual multiplication that has taken place in your own life. In the spaces below, fill in the names of those in your family of faith. See how God multiplies His work through the generations.

My Teacher/Role Model:

My Teacher's Student (your name):

My Students:

My Students' Students:

Now praise God for the leadership team He has built through you!

A LEADER'S LIFE

"For what profit is it to a man if he gains the whole world, and loses his own soul?"
—Matthew 16:26

A LEADER'S LIGHT

A Christian leader's journey begins at the time of her salvation and continues throughout her life. As a believer grows spiritually, she becomes better equipped to lead others and serve the Lord. Spiritual growth and development should continue throughout a believer's life. But it doesn't just happen! Priorities must be established to ensure that the believer stays committed to the Lord. In fact, a leader can become so busy doing the Lord's work that she loses touch with the Lord. As a Christian, you must keep your priorities centered around Him so that you will accomplish His will and you will enjoy the journey.

Before we begin this study of a leader's journey, specifically her priorities and life goals, take a few moments to evaluate your own priorities. **What are the most important priorities in your life at this time?**

How well are you managing the demands of your life priorities?

What happens when your priorities get out of control?

Most Christian women today have their plates full. We wear so many hats, juggle so many balls—all at the same time. There are responsibilities to our families, work, churches, and communities. We often have little time for

God and no time for self. It is difficult to balance priorities because of the screaming demands of others. When priorities get misplaced, life becomes stressful, frustrating, hopeless, and exhausting. We live in an exhausted world. To the question, "How are you?" most women today reply "Tired." Many women today are tired, but women in leadership are completely exhausted. If you want to survive this journey of life and enjoy yourself along the way, you must learn to prioritize your priorities and keep Jesus first place in your life. That is the only way for you to find rest and peace.

In her book, *Growing Weary Doing Good?*, Karla Worley gives personal testimony of the exhausting effect of a woman who spends all her time serving the Lord but no time with the Lord. That is why we have a generation of tired leaders. Women in leadership today need rest. But, as Karla says, "the church will not give you rest. All the conferences and retreats you may attend will not give you rest. Only Jesus is Rest. You cannot lighten your load by coming to meetings about Him. You must come to Him personally" (Worley, p. 8). To complete the journey, prevent burnout, and ensure effectiveness, a Christian leader must make her time with the Lord priority. It takes work and sacrifice, but it is worth it! There is great joy in the journey when you are enjoying intimate fellowship with the Lord.

HER LORD

The New Testament records three accounts of the sisters Mary and Martha. In each account, Jesus clearly taught about priorities. He identified the one thing that mattered, the first priority. **Read the passage in Luke 10:38-42 and describe the one commitment needed in the lives of all women.**

A Christian's first priority should be the Lord. A godly leader should seek first to spend time with the Lord. While service is important, it should result from an intimate encounter with the Lord. Jesus Himself said that He doesn't just want our work, He wants our hearts; He wants our devotion. God wants undistracted attention and unlimited time from us. He wants His children to start and end their days with Him. He wants us to put Him before other people and other things. He wants our total devotion.

Now read another account of Mary's devotion to Jesus in John 12:1-8. How did Jesus respond to Mary's anointing of His feet with the costly perfume?

Jesus used this opportunity to teach His disciples about devotion. A believer's number one priority should be the Lord. More than service to self or others, Christian leaders should love the Lord and spend time with Him in prayer and Bible study. Though the twelve disciples ministered with Jesus Christ Himself, they still misplaced their priorities. They focused on the Savior's work, not the Savior. They were too busy doing His will and not being still to know Him. The psalmist said it this way, "Be still, and know that I am God" (Ps. 46:10). The Lord doesn't call us to rest up in order to do more work. He wants us to be still, to rest, to be quiet so we can get to know Him. As Christian leaders, our first priority of every day should be our relationship with God.

I must confess, I have trouble being still. By my nature, I am an active, busy person. It is much easier for me to do and go than to sit and be still. But I have learned that those quiet moments alone with God are when God speaks to me about Himself. We fellowship together. It is refreshing to be still, but it is invigorating to know that He is God—to be fully aware of God. My days that begin in the presence of God are days that are filled with the power of God. I tank up on His presence when I prayerwalk in the mornings. In the quiet of those morning walks, I talk aloud to God, He talks back to me, and I am consciously aware of Him.

Recently a friend unexpectedly joined me as I was walking and praying. I have to admit, I was somewhat frustrated with the interruption. You see, I wasn't through with my prayertime. It pleased me to realize how precious my time alone with God was to me. While I love being with people, my walk was my time alone with God. We must keep that intimacy with the Lord our first priority. **How do you keep your relationship with the Lord in first place of your life? What do you do to keep your time with God as first priority? As you prayerfully consider your relationship with the Lord, renew your commitment to keep Him first place in your life.**

Leaders stay so busy doing good things that they often neglect their Lord, their families, and their own selves. When you keep the first things first, everything else seems to fall into place. If you keep God first place in your life, all the other things will find their places. Someone said it this way, "You must major on the majors, and not major on the minors." If you get out of balance, then you may lose it all. **Do you think that is what Jesus meant when He asked His disciples: "For what profit is it to a man if he gains the whole world, and loses his own soul? Or what will a man give in exchange for his soul?" (Matt. 16:26).**

Her Family

Power, position, and prestige are nothing compared to intimacy with the Father. Money, possessions, and things will vanish, but your relationship with God will endure. Don't let your work for the Lord interfere with your time with the Lord. Jesus may also have been warning His disciples not to let their work hurt their relationships with others. Leaders have a tendency to put work before people. How sad for a leader to gain success but lose her family!

Yes, God has called you to salvation and service, but He has also given you a family. You are the only wife your husband will ever have. You are the only mother your children will ever have. You are the only daughter your parents will ever have. You are the only sister your siblings will ever have. There will be other Sunday School teachers. There will be other Bible study leaders. But you have a responsibility assigned by God to care for your family, and that takes time. Don't become a leader who succeeds in her work but loses her family.

In the space provided below, write the names of your family members as a commitment to keep them as important priorities in your life.

My husband

My children

My mother

My father

My siblings

Other relatives

Aren't you grateful for your family? The best way for you to demonstrate your love and appreciation of them is with your time—give them the gift of yourself. As you do, you are teaching them to prioritize their priorities. You are teaching other women by example how "to love their husbands, to love their children" (Titus 2:4).

Unfortunately, we are living in a time when many Christian leaders have confused their priorities. They have put themselves or their work first and have lost their passion for the Lord and their families. Because of disobedience, they have left the Lord and neglected their families. Ministers divorce their wives. Leaders neglect their children. Christians reject their families. This is not God's plan. God wants all of His children to seek Him first and love each other. He wants leaders to do His work but not at the expense of their families. So every leader must cope with this tension—balancing the call of God with the other priorities of life. With the help of God, you can do His work and also be devoted to your family.

Read the following Scriptures as a reminder of the important emphasis God places on your family.

Genesis 2:18—I will make him a helper.

Ephesians 5:22—Wives submit to your own husbands, as to the Lord.

Deuteronomy 6:7—Teach God's Word to your children diligently.

Psalm 127:3-5—Children are a heritage from the Lord.

Exodus 20:12—Honor your father and mother.

God ordained the institution of marriage and He highly values the family, so as a godly leader you must nurture your family.

While the work God has called you to do is important, it is not the first priority of your life. Your journey will be filled with many ministry opportunities, but you must always keep Jesus and your family in their proper places. However, a responsible leader will also work tirelessly to do what God has called her to do. How can you balance your priorities in your journey as a leader without letting your work take control of your life? That will be a lifelong challenge for you.

One possible way to limit the intrusion of your work on all other areas of your life is to learn how to lead and not manage. It is a temptation for any leader to want to manage every little detail of the work. But it is particularly natural for a woman in leadership to involve herself in every aspect of the work. It is impossible to do all the work and keep your focus on the Lord and your family. The most valuable leadership lesson you can learn is how to lead and not manage. The work God has called you to should be accomplished through the help of others, not through your effort alone.

Jesus led His disciples. He didn't manage their every move. He cast the vision for His ministry, He trained them to minister, and He started the work. However, He gave them the freedom to manage the daily activities of the ministry. **Read Mark 10:32-34 to see how Jesus led His disciples.** Jesus led the way and He knew what would happen, but He allowed His disciples to make their own choices, to determine their own actions. Consider the way you accomplish your work—do you lead or do you manage? If you are managing every little detail, you will be unable to keep God's priorities and your team will be unable to work effectively.

HER WORK

Take a few minutes to read the advice given to Moses by his father-in-law Jethro in Exodus 18:17-27. How did Jethro's advice help Moses become a better leader? Identify a word or phrase of wisdom in each verse that teaches leaders to lead and not manage.

verse 17—

verse 18—

verse 19—

verse 20—

verse 21—

verse 22—

verse 23—

verse 24—

verse 25—

verse 26—

Jethro wisely advised his son-in-law Moses to lead and not manage. Moses was exhausted and discouraged because he had poured himself into his work and he wasn't succeeding. Jethro honestly informed Moses that his overworking was not good (v. 17). He was called to do a task that he couldn't do alone (v. 18). He was wearing out, burning out (v. 18). Jethro urged Moses to depend on God completely (v. 19). He also urged him to lead the people by teaching them the law of God (v. 20), and to find men who fear God to help him do the work (v. 21). Moses' helpers should handle all of the small matters while Moses was to give general guidance (v. 22). The ministry team would carry much of the burden of the hard work and help Moses endure (v. 23). Moses followed the counsel of Jethro and learned to lead. His men performed the small tasks and were blessed by their involvement in the work of God. That is a good lesson for leaders today—give general leadership but delegate daily responsibilities to others.

The debate between leadership and management continues in the fields of business, education, and religion. It is also a personal issue. How will you rank your priorities? Will you get bogged down in the details of your work? That's a leadership challenge I face personally. Because I am a "detail person," I could easily get caught up in the minutiae of my work and overlook the big picture. My daily decision must be to lead people, not manage the details. That is God's design for leaders (Ex. 18:23). In my work as coordinator of the women's ministry of my church, I must keep our purpose before us and give guidance to the ministry. There is no way I can manage every detail of every event. I must delegate those responsibilities to other team members and then allow them to perform their work. It is not easy for me, but I must let go. As I obey God's plan, I am better able to handle my life priorities, and they learn to use their spiritual gifts to serve the Lord. My leadership journey is an ongoing process of learning how to prioritize my time with the Lord, my family, and my work.

Let's return to the story about Mary of Bethany. She can teach us about proper priorities. She learned how to balance the many demands of her life and be blessed in the journey. Mary always put the Lord first in her life. Jesus acknowledged her faithfulness: "But one thing is needed, and Mary has chosen that good part, which will not be taken away from her" (Luke 10:42). She also loved her family, not just her brother, Lazarus, but also her sister, Martha. When Lazarus died, Mary wept uncontrollably and knew Jesus could have saved him. The Lord honored her faith in Him and love for her brother by raising Lazarus from the dead (John 11:43). Mary was also dedicated to her work. Before she anointed the feet of Jesus, Mary helped in preparing the meal (see John 12:2). She did not neglect her responsibility of work, but she kept her priorities prioritized.

A Christian leader will complete her journey and enjoy the trip, if she keeps her priorities straight—if she keeps her heart and life focused on the Lord; if she devotes herself to her family; and if she learns how to do her work well. If not, a leader's journey will be unproductive and exhausting. Let the words of Paul be a guide for you in your journey.

"Be assured that from the first day we heard of you, we haven't stopped praying for you, asking God to give you wise minds and spirits attuned to his will, and so acquire a thorough understanding of the ways in which God works. We pray that you'll live well for the Master, making him proud of you as you work hard in his orchard. As you learn more and more how God works, you will learn how to do your work. We pray that you'll have the strength to stick it out over the long haul—not the grim strength of gritting your teeth but the glory-strength that God gives. It is strength that endures the unendurable and spills over into joy, thanking the Father who makes us strong enough to take part in everything bright and beautiful that he has for us."
—Colossians 1:9-11 (*The Message*)

A LEADER'S LIFE

What priorities does your journey include? **List below the important priorities in your life; then ask God to help you know how to prioritize your priorities according to His will. Make this a daily prayer of commitment.**

"Well done, good and faithful servant; you were faithful over a few things, I will make you ruler over many things."—Matthew 25:21

A LEADER'S LIGHT

While a leader should not be motivated to seek rewards or praise, there are tremendous blessings poured out on the leader's life. There is great joy in accepting God's call and following His will. There is tremendous satisfaction in casting a vision and seeing it fulfilled. There is overwhelming gratitude when trained leaders work together to accomplish God's purpose. And there is heartfelt jubilation as supernatural work is accomplished. These are some of the greatest blessings of leadership.

But a leader also may receive praise—the praise of God, the praise of people, and even the praise of the world. Affirmation for leadership will often be expressed here on earth, but a leader's greatest praise will be voiced by God in heaven. What a joy to stand before the Lord and hear Him say, "Well done, good and faithful servant; you were faithful over a few things, I will make you ruler over many things" (Matt. 25:21). It is helpful for a leader to understand why praise is given and how to receive it. Praise blesses the giver and the receiver!

Let's take a few moments to study the context of Matthew 25 to understand the meaning of this lesson's focal verse. **Read the parable of the talents recorded in Matthew 25:14-30. Briefly summarize the parable in the space below.**

In this story, told by Jesus to teach a truth, a master gave talents or coins to his servants and then left them to handle the resources. The servant who received five talents doubled his possessions and the servant who received two talents gained two more. But the servant who received one talent hid the money and made no more. The master praised the two servants who wisely used their talents: "well done, good and faithful servant" (Matt. 25:21). The master rebuked the lazy servant who did not make a profit.

What is the lesson of this parable?

God, our Master, will praise us when we use the talents He has given us for good, and He will condemn us for squandering our talents. The Lord will reward our wise stewardship with more responsibility— "or to everyone who has, more will be given, and he will have abundance" (Matt. 25:29). What a wonderful promise to a faithful servant leader! But the Lord warns those who are not diligent: "But from him who does not have, even what he has will be taken away. And cast the unprofitable servant into the outer darkness." (Matt. 25:29-30). The unproductive leader will be condemned while the productive leader will be blessed.

In my own church, our pastor recently challenged the members to take what God has given them and multiply it for His glory. At the end of his message, he gave every person in the congregation a gold Sacagawea dollar, to represent the Greek *mina*, an ancient coin worth about 100 days' wages. He asked everyone to prayerfully consider investing their minas so that God's work could be blessed. During the next six weeks, church members creatively used their talents to multiply the minas. A teenage girl made beaded bracelets and the proceeds went to the "Mina Project." A preteen girls' Sunday School class pooled their minas to place a garage sale advertisement in the paper, and made over $800 for the "junk" they found cleaning their rooms. Several office workers created snack baskets for their break rooms at work; some teenage boys teamed up to take donut orders for Sunday School classes; and several children had lemonade stands in their neighborhoods. Several church members chose to invest other money and keep the original gold coin in their wallets as a constant reminder to use what God has given them. How exciting when at the end of six weeks proceeds were given back to the Lord through His church! On that day the minas returned with an increase of more than 20 times what was originally given out—and continued to return for several weeks. Those who were faithful with little were able to return much.

In this lesson, we will consider praise that is received by a leader. Commendation is given to leaders who excel. But God Himself glorifies the leader who obediently leads the people according to God's plan. Leaders must learn to graciously accept approval and generously extend exaltation. How comfortably do you receive praise and how frequently do you give it? One purpose of this Bible study is to help you understand the meaning of praise and how to receive it graciously.

All Christian leaders should treasure the praise of the Lord. When God says, "well done," to one of His children, He is honestly affirming the work that He knows was done. The Lord assures His children as they lead others—He gives a sense of satisfaction and accomplishment. He gives eternal rewards for faithful service in heaven—eternal crowns of glory. The ultimate praise for leadership is uttered by the Lord.

The Old Testament leader Nehemiah received praise for his effective leadership and sought the praise of God. Nehemiah served as cupbearer to the king of Persia (Neh. 1:11b). The Bible records his humble beginnings as well as his significant accomplishments. Like Esther, Nehemiah was used by God at "such a time as this" (Esth. 4:14) to help his people. He was a leader with extraordinary skills and abilities as well as a profound faith in God. Nehemiah was a leader of prayer, vision, and courage. He persisted under pressure, and he kept his priorities straight. He served with conviction, yet humbly worked alongside the others. No wonder Nehemiah was praised as a leader!

Christian leaders today can learn from Nehemiah's example. Nehemiah humbly received the accolades of the people, but he sincerely sought the praise of God. In the closing chapter of his book, Nehemiah concluded as he began—in prayer. His prayer was specific: "remember me, O my God, for good!" (Neh. 13:31). Four times Nehemiah asked God to remember him for his good—to pay attention to his successes, not failures. **Read the following verses, then complete the prayer of Nehemiah.**

Nehemiah 5:19— "Remember me, my God, for good."

Nehemiah 13:14— "Remember me, O my God, concerning this
_____."

Nehemiah 13:22— "Remember me, O my God, concerning this also, _____."

Nehemiah 13:31— "Remember me, O my God,
_____!"

What response did Nehemiah want to receive from God? He wanted God to be pleased with his efforts and praise him for his goodness. Can you think of examples of leaders who were praised by God?

The Bible records the praise of God for leaders who were faithful. Abraham was blessed by God as an obedient leader. The angel of the Lord spoke Abraham's praise: "Blessing I will bless you, and multiplying I will multiply your descendants....In your seed all the nations of the earth shall be blessed, because you have obeyed My voice" (Gen. 22:17-18). The Lord also promised Moses many blessings for faithfully leading the people of Israel into the Promised Land. In Deuteronomy 7:12-13, public praise is given to Moses: "Because you listen to these judgments, and keep and do them...He will love you and bless you and multiply you." Later, in the New Testament, two women were praised specifically for their faithfulness. In Hebrews 11, "the Hall of Heroes," both Sarah, wife of Abraham, and Rahab the harlot were remembered for their good testimony. The Word of God includes His praise for the faithfulness of His children.

Fern Nichols is a present-day example of a godly leader praised by the Lord. She was just one mom who asked God for another mom with whom she could pray for her children and their schools. As God provided and her passion for prayer developed, she founded Moms In Touch International to encourage other mothers to pray specifically and scripturally for their children and for schools. The vision of one mother has been blessed by God and today 25,000 schools in the United States have Moms In Touch groups praying for them. Fern's vision continues to increase, as she and others pray fervently that every school in the United States would be covered in prayer. God praised those who faithfully serve Him as He blessed their ministries.

THE PRAISE OF THE PEOPLE

An effective leader generously offers praise to others for their efforts and accomplishments. Praise not only motivates the people, but it affirms their actions and gives joy in their work. While ladies often have difficulty accepting praise, the praise itself is important in the ministry process. Personal praise of an individual lifts the spirits and public praise builds the team. Paul was a gracious leader who generously offered praise of others. **Read the following Scriptures where Paul acknowledges the efforts of co-laborers in the faith. Briefly write his words of praise so you will learn how to affirm others.**

Romans 16:1-2

Romans 16:3-5

Philippians 1:1, 3-6

Philemon 2-3

You must strive to praise and encourage those who work with you in the same way that Paul affirmed others. You must be their cheerleader. But as a leader, you must also learn how to accept praise from others.

My friend Karen Hayter, a licensed professional counselor, teaches about self-esteem. She says that many women have such poor self-concepts that they are unable to accept compliments. I remember two important teachings of a workshop she led on self-esteem: affirm people for *who* they are and not *what* they do, and say "thank you" without apology when someone praises you. What practical lessons! How do you respond when someone compliments you? Can you graciously reply "thank you" without an explanation or excuse? Leaders must learn to gratefully receive praise.

Refer back to the praise Paul gave to his coworkers. **How do you think these ladies responded to the kind words of Paul? While their actual responses were not recorded in Scripture, you can speculate how they responded from the atmosphere of the account. Record your thoughts below.**

Phoebe

Priscilla

Lydia

Apphia

Paul generously praised the work of others and they accepted his praise with grace. In the book, *Leadership and the One Minute Manager*, the authors include "Public Praisings" in the last pages (p. 106). They were not content to speak a word of thanks to those who helped in writing the book, they expressed public appreciation. They recorded their gratitude in print for all to read. Leaders should share public praisings of others and receive public praise with a smile and simple "thank you."

Philippians is a thank-you letter from Paul. While he does speak of the gospel, the cross, and the work of Christ, his words are filled with gratitude for the labors of the saints. **Read Philippians 1:3-11 below and circle words or phrases of praise.**

"I thank my God upon every remembrance of you, always in every prayer of mine making request for you all with joy, for your fellowship in the gospel from the first day until now, being confident of this very thing, that He who has begun a good work in you will complete it until the day of Jesus Christ; just as it is right for me to think this of you all, because I have you in my heart, inasmuch as both in my chains and in the defense and confirmation of the gospel, you all are partakers with me of grace. For God is my witness, how greatly I long for you all with the affection of Jesus Christ. And this I pray, that your love may abound still more and more in knowledge and all discernment, that you may approve the things that are excellent, that you may be sincere and without offense till the day of Christ, being filled with the fruits of righteousness which are by Jesus Christ, to the glory and praise of God."—Philippians 1:3-11

Learn to generously express praise to others and graciously receive praise for yourself. A leader's praise may come from the Lord, other people, or the world.

THE PRAISE OF THE WORLD

When a leader leads well, that leader may be recognized by the world. Awards and gifts are presented for years of service. Testimonials and receptions publicly acknowledge personal efforts. While the world most often celebrates the sensational or publicizes the tragic, there are times that even the national media give attention to the works of the Lord and His children. **Can you think of godly leaders or a Christian ministry that has been praised by the world? List their names below with a brief description of the praise they received.**

President Jimmy Carter was proclaimed by the media "the born-again President of the United States" because he was vocal with his faith. He continues to receive public praise for his humanitarian works through Middle East negotiations and Habitat for Humanity. He continues to be active in public service and is praised for his unselfish work. The world has acknowledged his many positive contributions as president and as a personal volunteer. President Carter is also an example to other leaders of one who graciously receives praise.

88

On a personal note, I can remember my surprise as a high school senior when I was recognized by my classmates as "Miss John F. Kennedy High School." I realized for the first time that my godly character and Christian behavior was respected by my peers. They selected me as the most outstanding student and praised me for my leadership in school. The world does notice the life of a godly leader. And while there may be ridicule or teasing, there is often deep respect for spiritual convictions and commitments. The praise of the world is a special treasure because it is often unexpected and unprecedented. Christian leaders must be aware that the world is watching as they lead. And if they lead effectively, the world will enthusiastically cheer on the successes.

Deborah, a leader of Israel, was praised by God, praised by her people, and praised by the world. She obediently followed the direction of the Lord and led the Israelites as a prophetess and judge (Judg. 4:4). She was the only woman in Scripture to be elevated to a position of power by the common consent of her peers. What an expression of praise! **Read Judges 4:14-16 to understand the support given by everyone toward Deborah's leadership.** Speaking God's Word with confidence, Deborah gave direction to Barak who led the armies to defeat their enemy. Praise by others is often reflected in their willingness to follow a leader even if it might lead to death.

While praise should not be the primary motivation of ministry, it is truly a blessing of faithful service. As a leader learns to receive and give praise, she is modeling the life of Christ who affirmed His children and was adored by others. A godly leader will humbly accept the praise of others and give all the glory of success to God. As you develop skills as a Christian leader, learn to graciously receive, genuinely reflect, and generously return the praise of God and others!

How have you received praise for your leadership? Take a few minutes to consider the ways that God, people, and the world have affirmed you. **List these expressions of praise below.**

God—

People—

The World—

Now give all the glory to God for what He has done through you.

89

 ESSON TWELVE | A LEADER'S LEGACY

"I have fought the good fight, I have finished the race, I have kept the faith."
—2 Timothy 4:7

A LEADER'S
LIGHT

In the past few weeks you have been studying about leadership—not dictatorial leadership, but servant leadership. You have examined who a leader is and what she does. You have affirmed the call to leadership and the vision for leadership. You have evaluated the personal life, positional power, and particular styles of a leader while also acknowledging limitations and challenges of leadership. In the last three lessons, you have focused on the leadership team as well as the leader's journey and praise. Now it is time to consider a leader's legacy. What will you, the leader, leave behind? What convictions will you pass down? What will be remembered about you?

Each leader begins creating her legacy the day she begins serving in a leadership role. That is true of all leaders. The legacy begins with the leadership. It is important for a leader to determine what she wants her legacy to be before she begins to lead.

What do you want your legacy to be? As a college student attending a leadership conference, I was asked to write my obituary. What an unusual request of a young woman! But our leaders were challenging us to plan ahead for the things we wanted to accomplish as a leader and then look back over that legacy. Let's take a few minutes to do that now. In the space provided below, write what you would like your legacy to be. Feel free to include personal traits as well as leadership accomplishments. **Write your own obituary**.

While it is impossible to know with certainty what you will accomplish, it is important to plan your legacy. I have heard some godly leaders respond humbly to a public recognition: "There is no way any human being could be that great, certainly not me," or "I am so undeserving of this praise and applause." After numerous testimonies of accomplishment, at a retirement dinner, one leader humorously responded "it sounds like I'm dead. No one would say those nice things to anyone who is alive!" Well, many of us will never live to see our dreams fulfilled or goals accomplished. But others will celebrate with joy their accomplishments. We will not hear the eulogy at our funeral or read our own obituary. Instead our legacy will be revealed as we stand before God. As a person and as a leader you have already begun determining your legacy and will be building your legacy until the day you die.

In this final lesson, we will examine three dimensions of a leader's legacy. Though many other memories will remain, every leader will leave a legacy—a good one or a bad one, a fading one or a lasting one. My prayer is that your leadership will be good and godly, lasting and even everlasting. A godly leader who leaves a lasting legacy can say:

"I have done God's will."
"I have accomplished God's work."
"I have prepared God's workers."

I HAVE DONE GOD'S WILL

Paul the apostle wrote honestly about his successes and failures in ministry. He confessed his personal weaknesses to God and acknowledged his strengths from God. In his second letter to Timothy, he had the opportunity to write his own obituary. He knew that his death was imminent, so he reflected back on his ministry. We find Paul's valedictory speech in 2 Timothy 4:6-8, his farewell address to his young son in the faith and to other followers of Christ. Read 2 Timothy 4:6-8 carefully. What do you think Paul meant when he said, "I have fought the good fight, I have finished the race, I have kept the faith"? **Write your paraphrase here**.

Paul reflected on his life and ministry—he had fought a good fight. Truly, Paul's life was a fight—he was challenged from every side as he preached the gospel. He experienced the suffering and imprisonment of a soldier in battle, and he concluded that his battles had been worth it. It had been a "good fight," a fight for good. His cause was a worthy cause—the cause of the gospel. He said it this way in 1 Timothy 6:12: "Fight the good fight of faith, lay hold on eternal life, to which you were also called and have confessed the good confession in the presence of many witnesses." His fight was for the faith.

In his second phrase, Paul professed that he had "finished the race" (2 Tim. 4:7). He knew his life was coming to an end and that his ministry was almost over. Written from prison in Rome, 2 Timothy was Paul's last epistle. He was completing his race of life. Despite many obstacles along the way, Paul persevered in his faith and in his ministry. Throughout his race, Paul kept his eye on the finish line not on the sidelines. He was not distracted by his personal ambitions or the criticism of others. He stayed focused on the goal—the pursuit of God's will. Paul classified his goal to the Galatians: "I… communicated to them that gospel which I preach among the Gentiles, but privately to those who were of reputation, lest by any means I might run, or had run, in vain" (Gal. 2:2). To the Philippians he spoke with conviction: "Holding fast the word of life, so that I may rejoice in the day of Christ that I have not run in vain or labored in vain" (Phil. 2:16). At the end of his life, Paul could honestly conclude that he had finished the race God had set before him.

Paul's last phrase affirmed his conviction—"I have kept the faith." Even in his trials, Paul had maintained his trust in God. He was confident in God and completely trusted in His promises. Read his statement again in 1 Timothy 6:12: "Fight the good fight of faith, lay hold of eternal life." Paul's faith had sustained him and his salvation was sure. He knew that his eternity would be spent with God in heaven because of his personal faith. He could also stand before God as an obedient child who served faithfully.

Paul's obituary in 2 Timothy 4:7 can be summarized simply: "I have done God's will." I sincerely desire to speak those same words with confidence as I come to the end of my life and ministry. Do you? What a powerful leadership legacy to say, "I have done His will."

A godly man who served for years at our seminary fought a valiant fight against cancer. Though in constant pain, he completed the writing of a Sunday School series before his death. He was determined to live long enough to complete the work God had called him to do. When his work was completed, his body grew weaker, but he experienced the peace of the Lord. As he died, he could say like the apostle Paul: "I have fought the good fight, I have finished the race, I have kept the faith" (2 Tim. 4:7). That faithful servant of God left a lasting legacy. Each Christian leader should strive to be faithful like Paul and say, at the end of life, "I have done God's will." A leader of legacy should also be able to say, "I have accomplished His work."

I Have Accomplished God's Work

God calls all His children to do His work. While the work for every person is different, all the work is for God's purpose and to bring glory to Him. **What has God called you to do? It might be difficult, but in one sentence, try to summarize the work God has called you to do.**

Jesus came to earth as a man to do His Father's work. Though His ministry on earth was brief, His mission was complete. In fact, it was through His death that Jesus accomplished our salvation and finished His work. Read John 17:1-5 to remember the last words of Jesus. **What did Jesus say to His Father about His work? Write your answer here.**

Even before His crucifixion and resurrection, Jesus concluded that His work on earth had been accomplished. His Father's plan had been fulfilled: to bring salvation to the world through Jesus Christ. And the Father had been glorified—through the obedient life and faithful ministry of His Son, Jesus. Now Jesus anticipated the glory to come in heaven with the Father. Because He was God in the flesh, Jesus could perfectly fulfill His mission from God.

Mother Teresa was a little-known Catholic nun who became known to the whole world. Called to help the poor of India, she worked tirelessly to provide food, clothing, and shelter for the less fortunate. Her work with the sick and abandoned was spread through her work with other nuns. Her humanitarian efforts changed not only India but also the entire world. Mother Teresa, a frail, humble servant, cared for others until the time of her death. Because of her sacrificial effort, Mother Teresa could say, "I have accomplished God's work."

Can you think of some things you have done for the Lord? What work for the Lord have you accomplished? List a few of your ministry accomplishments in the margin.

Now ask yourself if your works accomplished God's work. Yes ___ or No ___. Have your works brought glory to God? If so, you can respond like Jesus: "I have glorified you on the earth" (John 17:4). If not, you can ask forgiveness from God and seek to do His will from now on. Then you can await the glory of the Lord in heaven and you can say to Him, "I have accomplished Your work."

A godly leader leaves a lasting legacy when she has done God's will, accomplished His work, and prepared His workers. God's work on earth will not continue unless you have trained others to follow. As you have instructed by word and example, you are equipping the saints to do the work of the ministry (Eph. 4:12). There is no greater calling than the call to equip others.

Paul taught about this equipping ministry in Ephesians 4:1-16. Read this powerful passage to remember why God calls and gifts His children. Though God wants all His children to spread the gospel and train Christians, He has truly gifted some ministers to equip leaders. What a precious privilege it is to prepare His workers!

Do you know someone who is especially gifted in training others? While I know many effective teachers, my brother-in-law, Paige Patterson, is truly gifted in equipping leaders. He began his teaching ministry when my husband, Chuck, was a young boy. Because he wanted Chuck to grow up to serve the Lord, Paige talked with him about doctrine, challenged him to learn, and encouraged him in ministry. They have spent hours together discussing matters of faith. Paige has shared his experience with Chuck and countless other young men committed to ministry. In 1999, when he was recognized as president of the Southern Baptist Convention, the moderator asked all those ministers who had been mentored by Paige Patterson to come forward. My husband, Chuck, was among the scores of men to publicly acknowledge the influence of this one godly man.

God has given my husband and me the passion for preparing His workers. In 1978, we developed our ministry called Innovative Evangelism. Not knowing all that God had in store for us, we adopted Ephesians 4:12 as our biblical foundation. Even as students ourselves, we knew that God wanted us to teach others. God has blessed our desire as today both of us are actively involved in training leaders for ministry. As president of the New Orleans Baptist Theological Seminary, Chuck is training men and women to fulfill the Great Commission and the Great Commandments through the local church and its ministries. I am training women to minister to other women through the Women's Ministry Program at the seminary. Chuck and I desire to stand before God one day and say: "I have prepared Your workers."

In another one of his epistles, Paul challenged the Christians in Corinth to serve the Lord faithfully and train others diligently for kingdom work. In fact, he concluded that the greatest commendations of a leader are the lives of those she influences. Paul told the Corinthians: "You are our epistle written in our hearts, known and read by all men; clearly you are an epistle of Christ, ministered by us, written not with ink but by the Spirit of the living God, not on tablets of stone, but on tablets of flesh, that is of the heart" (2 Cor. 3:2-3). **What does that passage mean to you?**

I HAVE PREPARED GOD'S WORKERS

In her book, *Leadership Legacies*, Catherine Allen suggests some rules for mentoring. Let me summarize a few of her suggestions for leaders who want to leave a lasting legacy.

1. Help someone else learn what God has taught you.
2. Notice budding leaders, those with obvious potential.
3. Allow access to your life, your time, your work, your history.
4. Give praise and positive feedback.
5. Suggest opportunities for enlarging the horizons and the heritage.

What practical suggestions! As leaders in ministry, we must be investing our lives in the future as we train the next generation.

This Bible study has been about servant leadership, the model exemplified by Jesus, not the model taught by the world. It has been my prayer for you to affirm who you are in Christ—a born-again believer and a committed leader. Your journey through Scripture has described servant leadership and identified the leader's calling. You have clarified your vision and committed to a godly lifestyle. You have examined the strengths and weaknesses of a leader's power and learned about the various styles of leadership. You have acknowledged the limitations and challenges faced by a leader and you have explored the ways to develop a leadership team. You have traveled a leader's journey and heard a leader's praise. In this final lesson, you have been challenged to leave a godly leadership legacy. This Bible study has been a guide for you. But you must apply the biblical lessons.

Now you must decide: will you be a servant leader? When God called you to salvation, you received His gift of new life. When He called you to service, you followed His direction. As He calls you to lead others, you have the choice of how to lead. Will you choose to lead as Christ led? Or will you follow the examples of the world? It is my prayer that you will always be a servant leader. Christ came not to be served but to serve. You have been called to lead not for your own benefit, but for the benefit of others. There is great glory in servant leadership! Glory to God and His faithful children together for all eternity.

A LEADER'S LIFE

Read the following statements and respond honestly.
I have done God's will. ___ yes ___no. Why or why not?

I have accomplished God's work. ___ yes ___ no. Why or why not?

I have prepared God's workers. ___ yes ___ no. Why or why not?

Close in prayer asking God to help you leave a lasting legacy.

GROUP TEACHING GUIDE

This section includes some teaching suggestions for the small group leader. It also provides a format for the discussion time and a typical schedule for a one-hour session. Feel free to use the suggestions in part or as a whole. However, let the Holy Spirit lead your group discussion and make any appropriate changes. These are simply teaching helps.

A Leader's Work

Prayer Time (5 minutes)
As you begin the prayertime, ask the group members to name some world, national, local, and church leaders. Spend some time in prayer for each of these leaders.

Review (5 minutes)
Spend a few minutes reviewing the purpose and format of this Bible study. Welcome new members and answer any questions about the format.

Introduction (5 minutes)
Ask group members to think about leadership from a personal and positional perspective. All of us are leaders personally—in the home, church, and community. Some are leaders with a position of responsibility. Discuss the difference between these two types of leadership.

Group Discussion (40 minutes)
Read aloud several of the definitions of leadership. Ask group members to share other definitions of leadership or their own definitions.
• Discuss whether or not you think leaders are born or trained. Share examples of both types of leaders.
• Ask someone to read Exodus 18:19-23. Discuss Jethro's leadership advice to Moses.

LESSON ONE

• Allow time for members to reread John 13:14-17. Then ask them to describe Jesus' model of servanthood. How does the leadership model of Jesus differ from the model of the world?

• Lead the group in reading aloud Mark 10:43-45. Discuss how you plan to lead by serving. Refer to "A Leader's Life" at the end of Lesson One.

Closing (5 minutes)

Encourage each member of the group to spend time in prayer personally. Make a commitment to servant leadership like Jesus. Conclude the prayer time by reading aloud Mark 10:45.

LESSON TWO

A Leader's Calling

Prayer Time (5 minutes)

Spend a few moments in silent prayer asking God to clarify the call in your life. Recommit yourself to fulfilling that special call.

Review (5 minutes)

Review some definitions of leadership and mention any new insights gained since last week. Encourage group members to continue to develop their own definitions of leadership.

Introduction (5 minutes)

Briefly discuss what is meant by "the call." Ask members to share a specific call by God on their lives.

Group Discussion (40 minutes)

• Ask four different members to read the definitions of "call" included in the Bible study. Encourage each one to use her meaning of call in a sentence correctly.

• Have the group members read aloud the Scripture references about the call. Discuss what each passage teaches about the call from God. Focus especially on 2 Timothy 1:8-11, this week's focal Scripture.

• Allow time for group members to describe their fellowship with God. You may ask these questions to start the discussion: How much time do you spend with God? How much time have you spent with Him today? How close is your relationship with God?

• Enlist one member to read aloud 1 John 1:1-7. Discuss what this passage teaches about fellowship with others.

• Guide the group in listing the responsibilities of the call to servant leadership. Write on the board some specific guidelines for leaders to follow.

• Take a few moments to discuss the responsibility of "the call." How does God hold us accountable?

Closing (5 minutes)
Read Ephesians 4:1-6 as a challenge to remain faithful to God's calling. Pray specifically for members of the group who have been called by God.

A Leader's Vision

Prayer Time (5 minutes)
Read the focal Scripture aloud—"Where there is no vision, the people perish" (Proverbs 29:18 KJV). Then ask every member to pray for church, political, and other leaders to have a clear vision from God so that the people will not perish.

Review (5 minutes)
Remind the members of the purpose and responsibility of a leader's calling. Ask them to share any confirmation this week of God's calling on their lives.

Introduction (5 minutes)
Briefly discuss what members understand about vision. You may want to discuss sight or eye vision as well as perception or foresight—the vision necessary for leadership.

Group Discussion (40 minutes)
• Read the four qualities of a leader suggested by Hunt and Hutcheson. Ask group members if they agree that vision is the most important quality of leadership. Why or why not?
• Ask one person to read Nehemiah 2:11-20. Discuss the visionary leadership of Nehemiah.
• Discuss how visionary foresight is reflected in Christian leaders today. Discuss some creative ways Christians are leading today. Discuss why you think visionary understanding is essential to effective leadership.
• After the discussion, see if members would like to share their understanding of vision. They may want to add to their earlier definition.

Closing (5 minutes)
As you close, ask this pointed question: has God given you a clear vision for leadership? Allow time to contemplate the question. Then close in prayer.

Prayer Time (5 minutes)

Encourage each group member to pray with a partner. Suggest that they share personal praise and specific prayer requests. Close the prayertime with a brief sentence prayer.

Review (5 minutes)

Briefly discuss a leader's vision—foresight, imagination, and understanding. Why are each necessary for effective leadership?

Introduction (5 minutes)

Lead the ladies in discussing discipline. Ask them: How hard is it to discipline your children? How difficult is it to be disciplined? Briefly introduce the topic of discipline—personal, mental and spiritual—as it will be discussed in this lesson.

Group Discussion (40 minutes)

• Ask the group members to discuss character. After sharing personal insights ask someone to read John Bowling's definition of character included in Lesson Four.

• Read 1 Timothy 3:8-13 aloud then ask the group to discuss important personal traits of a leader. Why is personal discipline necessary for a leader?

• Discuss the role of mental discipline in a leader's life. Suggest specific steps toward mental and emotional health.

• Ask the ladies to read together the fruit of the Spirit from Galatians 5:22-23. Allow time for them to share their descriptions of each Christian virtue. Why is spiritual discipline necessary for a Christian leader?

• Review the five suggestions for developing personal, mental, and spiritual discipline. Ask the group members if they agree or disagree. Why or why not?

Closing (5 minutes)

Just in case the ladies were unable to do so in advance, allow time for them individually to answer the three questions in "A Leader's Life." Close with a prayer of renewal and commitment.

A Leader's Power

Prayer Time (5 minutes)

Read aloud the prayer of King David found in Psalm 51:10-12. Lead the group in praying for God to keep them close to Him and clean in heart.

Review (5 minutes)

Ask individuals to share one thing that God has taught them about the discipline needed in a leader's life—personal, mental, and spiritual.

Introduction (5 minutes)

Introduce the discussion of power. Ask the group members what they think about the power of leadership. Is it good or bad? Why?

Group Discussion (40 minutes)

• Brainstorm some definitions of the word "power." Then read the quote about power by Peter Koestenbaum provided in this lesson.

• Allow a few minutes for group members to review the story of King David in 2 Samuel 11 and then discuss how he abused his power.

• Clarify for the group who the source of power is for Christian leaders. Remind them of the many ways the Holy Spirit works in the life of the leader. Read aloud several Scriptures from John noted in the lesson.

• Make a list of ways that a leader can use her power for the good of others to glorify God. Then discuss the suggestions in the book.

• Ask the group to share experiences when the Holy Spirit empowered them supernaturally. Remind them of the potential of the Holy Spirit to work in their lives.

Closing (5 minutes)

Conclude by asking the group to share how they have used their power for the good of others and to glorify God. Enlist one member to close in prayer.

A Leader's Style

Prayertime (5 minutes)

As individuals enter, ask them to write a personal prayer request on a blank 3-by-5 index card. Exchange the prayer requests and allow a few minutes for the ladies to pray aloud about their specific prayer request. Then you can close the prayertime.

Review (5 minutes)

Remind the group members of the true source of a leader's power. Solicit testimonies of how God has empowered them to lead even this week.

Introduction (5 minutes)

Ask the group members: What do you think of when you hear the word "style"? How does a person's style impact her life and work? Focus their attention on leadership style, not clothing style.

Group Discussion (40 minutes)

• Briefly discuss why an understanding of personality styles is helpful to a leader. Specific examples may be shared.

• Read aloud the descriptors of the four personality types included in this lesson. Ask members to identify their own personality styles and how they affect their leadership abilities.

• Discuss the leadership styles introduced by Ken Blanchard. Pose this question. "Is there a leadership style you desire to develop?" Why?

• List on the board the characteristics of Deborah's leadership. Discuss how she used these abilities to lead her people.

• Take a few minutes to evaluate the styles of leaders today. You may choose to discuss church leaders or political leaders. However, be careful not to criticize but to affirm specific leadership styles.

Closing (5 minutes)

Guide the ladies in a closing prayertime. First, ask them to thank God for their own unique personality styles. Then encourage them to seek God's help to increase their leadership strengths and decrease their weaknesses. Close by suggesting that each one recommit herself to be a godly leader.

LESSON SEVEN

A Leader's Limitations

Prayer Time (5 minutes)

Allow a few minutes of silent prayer for group members to confess any sin to God. Close the prayertime by asking God to forgive sins of omission and commission so that He can work through the lives of these leaders.

Review (5 minutes)

Last week's lesson focused on a leader's style. Briefly review how personality types and leadership styles affect a leader's work.

Introduction (5 minutes)

As you introduce the topic of a leader's limitations, slowly read aloud the five statements by John Maxwell included in the opening discussion. Ask members to consider what a leader's limitations are.

Group Discussion (40 minutes)

• Call on a group member to read 1 Corinthians 9:27 then discuss how Paul tried to overcome his personal limitations to become a godly leader.

• List on the board suggested skills needed for leadership. Discuss how the lack of those skills limits leadership.

• Identify the seven perils of leadership cited by J. Oswald Sanders, then have volunteers read the following Scriptures which warn about these weaknesses—Proverbs 16:5; Proverbs 14:16; Proverbs 14:30; 1 Corinthians 3:5-7; Luke 8:43-48; 1 Samuel 24:16-22; and Luke 10:20.

• Provide 3-by-5 index cards for group members to write down a personal failure. Then as you read aloud 1 John 1:9, ask them to tear up the cards in an act symbolic of God's forgiveness.

• Ask the group if they know of leaders who experienced personal failures or had children who were prodigal. How did their failures impact their leadership? What can those leaders learn from Eli and Samuel?

Closing (5 minutes)

As you close in prayer, ask those who feel led to pray aloud to lift up the fallen who were mentioned in this discussion. Then ask God to protect Christian leaders and help them recognize their own personal limitations.

A Leader's Challenges

Prayertime (5 minutes)

As you begin the prayertime, ask group members to share the names of Christian leaders they know who are facing challenges. Spend time in prayer for those leaders and pray for God's guidance when facing challenges.

Review (5 minutes)

Ask group members to remember some personal limitations and weaknesses that are common among leaders. Remind them that the Holy Spirit can overcome all those weaknesses with His strength.

Introduction (5 minutes)

Introduce this week's lesson by asking participants to brainstorm types of leadership challenges. On the board, list those challenges under one of the three headings: Difficult People, Tough Circumstances, Hard Work. Conclude the introduction by stating this truth—all leaders will face challenges at some time in ministry.

Group Discussion (40 minutes)

• Take time to read and discuss John Maxwell's five people limitations. Ask the group members if they agree or disagree with his conclusions.

• Write the names for the six types of difficult souls suggested by Calvin Miller on small pieces of paper. Fold the papers then ask each group member to select one. As she identifies a difficult person, read the description from the lesson. Briefly discuss biblical ways to handle each one.

• Seek a volunteer to read 1 Samuel 25:2-3, then discuss how Abigail handled her tough circumstances. Can you think of how Abigail can teach Christian leaders to face tough times? Discuss.

• Suggest that the group divide up into pairs. By twos, honestly discuss how you receive personal criticism. Then discuss what God needs to teach you about accepting criticism.

• Ask the group: What does Proverbs 31:10-31 teach about handling stress and burnout? How can this biblical character encourage leaders?

Closing (5 minutes)

Conclude the Bible study with praise. Read Psalm 46 then close in prayer by thanking God for His help in times of trouble.

LESSON NINE

A Leader's Team

Prayertime (5 minutes)

Hold hands in the group and ask each group member to pray for the person on her right. Ask the person on your right to begin, then you can close, the prayertime.

Review (5 minutes)

Remind the group of common leadership challenges discussed last week. Ask if anyone thought of additional leadership challenges since the previous discussion.

Introduction (5 minutes)

Divide the group into two teams. Give them two minutes to write down as many difficult types of teams as possible. You may want to give a prize to the team with the largest number. Then share the types of teams suggested and discuss why teams are important.

Group Discussion (40 minutes)

• Ask three group members to read the following passages of Scripture–Matthew 10:1-4; Mark 3:13-19; and Luke 6:12-16. Then discuss how Jesus selected His twelve disciples and why.

• Review the suggestions given in this week's lesson for finding a leadership team. See if group members can add other ways to find members for a leadership team.

• Enlist a group member to read 1 Timothy 4:11-16. As a group, list the six training instructions given by Paul to Timothy.

• Write on the board the name of each group member. Ask each person to identify one person they have trained for a leadership position and write that name beside hers. See if any member can identify someone trained by their trainee and write the name of this third-generation leader. Together you can visualize the multiplication of leaders just from your group.

• Discuss Gene Wilkes' five-step plan for equipping others for ministry–EQUIP. It is summarized in this week's lesson. Ask the group to discuss how they are equipping future generations for leadership.

Closing (5 minutes)

As a Bible study team, close in prayer by expressing praise for those people who have encouraged you and trained you for leadership. Then ask God to use you to train future leaders.

A Leader's Journey

Prayer Time (5 minutes)

Allow a few minutes for each group member to spend time in reflection and prayer. Suggest that they remember their life's journey, thanking God for the mountain and valley experiences.

Review (5 minutes)

Read 2 Timothy 2:1-7 aloud and review Paul's instructions to young Timothy about multiplying the ministry team. Discuss how Christian leaders can pass on a legacy of godly leadership.

Introduction (5 minutes)

Take a few minutes to briefly summarize your own life journey including highlights such as birth, childhood, conversion, education, family, and ministry. Stress how life is a personal journey filled with blessings and challenges.

Group Discussion (40 minutes)

• Encourage group members to draw a timeline of their life, including dates of major events. Here is an example of types of life events:

19__	19__	19__	19__	19__	20__
Birth	Graduation	Marriage	Child's Birth	Ministry	Present

Ask them to share how they feel at this time about their life journey.
• Focus now on the journey of a leader. What should a Christian leader's priorities be? Discuss.
• Ask a volunteer to read the account of Mary of Bethany in John 12:1-8. Discuss what Christian leaders can learn from Mary's relationship with her Lord.
• Before the Bible study, write these five Scripture references on separate pieces of paper:
Genesis 2:18; Ephesians 5:22; Deuteronomy 6:7; Psalm 127:3-5; and Exodus 20:12. Hand the Scriptures out to different group members. Ask them to read the Scripture, then summarize what God thinks about the priority of family.
• Briefly explain the advice given by Jethro to his son-in-law Moses in Exodus 18:17-27. Ask the group members to suggest words or phrases of wisdom from the Scripture passage.

Closing (5 minutes)

Close by reading Colossians 1:9-11 from *The Message,* then pray asking God to guide each group member through her journey of life and leadership.

LESSON ELEVEN

A Leader's Praise

Prayertime (5 minutes)

Write the word *PRAISE* on the board from top to bottom. Ask group members to share some praises that begin with each letter of the word *PRAISE* (examples: Provision, Redemption, All-Powerful, Intimacy, Sovereignty, and Encouragement). Close with a brief prayer.

Review (5 minutes)

Briefly discuss with the group some biblical priorities in a leader's journey—her Lord, her family, and her work. You can review last week's lesson for some specifics.

Introduction (5 minutes)

Begin to introduce this study with a brief definition of praise—"giving God His due." Then ask these rhetorical questions: Who is to praise God? Where do you praise God? How do you praise God? What do you praise God for? When do you praise God? Why do you praise God? Explain that this week's lesson will discuss the praise given to a leader.

Group Discussion (40 minutes)

• Summarize the parable of the talents in Matthew 25:14-30. Ask someone to read and explain this week's focal verse–Matthew 25:21. Then discuss a few lessons learned from this parable.

• Review the prayer of Nehemiah 13:14-31. Nehemiah asked God to remember his good works and praise him. Do you desire the praise of God? Why?

• Explain to the group the importance of giving praise to people—it exemplifies Christ, expresses self, and encourages others. Allow a few minutes for group members to voice public praisings for specific people.

• Discuss how Christian leaders today are regarded by the world. Are they praised or ridiculed? Give some examples.

• Allow a few minutes for group members to complete this week's "A Leader's Life." After completion of this activity, ask individuals to share how they have been praised for their leadership.

Closing (5 minutes)

Conclude by reading together the focal verse, Matthew 25:21. Read it several times and encourage group members to memorize it. Then ask a volunteer to close in prayer.

A Leader's Legacy

Prayer Time (5 minutes)

Lead the group in a corporate prayertime. Ask members to pray a sentence prayer as they feel led, thanking God for their personal legacy of faith.

Review (5 minutes)

Review the focal Scripture verse from last week, Matthew 25:21. Ask several group members to paraphrase the verse in their own words.

Introduction (5 minutes)

Introduce this study by discussing what a legacy is—a gift passed down from one person to another. Then ask group members to share what they would like their personal legacy to be.

Group Discussion (40 minutes)

• Write the following Scripture references on the board: Galatians 2:2; Philippians 2:16; 1 Timothy 6:12; and 2 Timothy 4:7. Ask volunteers to read them aloud to identify how Paul felt about his work. He concluded: "I have done His will."

• Ask: What did Jesus say about His work? Then read John 17:1-5 aloud. Jesus could truthfully say, "I have accomplished His work."

• Read Ephesians 4:11-16, then write verse 12 on the board one word at a time. Ask the group to read verse 12 in unison. Summarize the farewell of faithful Christian leaders saying, "I have prepared His workers."

• Read the rules for mentoring suggested by Catherine Allen in *Leadership Legacies*. As a group, discuss why you agree or disagree with these statements.

• Read aloud Paul's closing comment on his life and legacy in 2 Timothy 4:7. Then give the group a few minutes for each person to write her own statement about her life and legacy.

Closing (5 minutes)

Ask each group member to write a prayer of commitment, dedicating her life and leadership to the Lord and asking God to build a lasting legacy of faith.

BIBLIOGRAPHY

Adams, Chris, ed., *Women Reaching Women: Beginning and Building a Growing Women's Enrichment Ministry.* (Nashville: Life Way Press, 1997).

Adams, Chris, ed.. *Transformed Lives: Taking Women's Ministry to the Next Level.* (Nashville: LifeWay Press, 1999).

Alexander, Donald L., ed. *Christian Spirituality.* (Downers Grove, IL: InterVarsity Press, 1998).

Allen, Catherine B. with Alma Hunt. *Leadership Legacies: Lessons for Christian Women Leaders.* (Birmingham, AL: Women's Missionary Union, 2000).

Arnold, Jeffrey. *Seven Traits of A Successful Leader.* (Colorado Springs: NavPress, 1997).

Augsburger, David. *Caring Enough to Confront.* (Ventura, CA: Regal Books, 1981).

Bailey, Robert W. *Coping with Stress in the Minister's Home.* (Nashville: Broadman Press, 1979).

Beausay, William II. *The People Skills of Jesus.* (Nashville: Thomas Nelson, 1997).

Biehl, Bobb. *Stop Setting Goals If You Would Rather Solve Problems.* (New York: Ballantine Books, 1996).

Blanchard, Kenneth, et al. *Leadership and the One Minute Manager.* (New York: William Morrow, 1985).

Blanchard, Ken and Spencer Johnson. *The One Minute Manager.* (New York: Berkley Books, 1982).

Bolton, Robert. *People Skills.* (New York: AMACOM, 1986).

Bolton, Robert and Dorothy Grover Bolton. *People Styles at Work: Making Bad Relationships Good and Good Relationships Better.* (New York: AMACOM, 1996).

Bowling, John C. *Grace-Full Leadership.* (Kansas City: Beacon Hill Press, 2000).

Bramson, Robert M. *Coping With Difficult People.* (New York: Dell Publishing, 1981).

Branden, Nathaniel. *The Power of Self-Esteem.* (Deerfield Beach, FL: Health Communications, 1992).

Brill, Naomi. *Working with People: The Helping Process.* (White Plains, NY: Longman Publishers, 1995).

Briner, Bob. *One Minute Bible: Women in Leadership.* (Nashville: Broadman & Holman, 1999).

Briner, Bob and Ray Pritchard. *More Leadership Lessons of Jesus.* (Nashville: Broadman & Holman, 1998).

Brinkman, Rick, Rick Kirschner, and Rich Brinkman. *Dealing with People You Can't Stand: How to Bring Out the Best in People at Their Worst.* (New York: McGraw-Hill, 1994).

Briscoe, Jill, et al. *Designing Effective Women's Ministries.* (Grand Rapids: Zondervan, 1995).

Burns, James MacGregor. *Leadership.* (New York: Harper & Row, 1989).

Clinton, Robert. *The Making of a Leader.* (Colorado Springs: NavPress, 1988).

Clowse, Barbara Barksdale. *Women, Decision Making, and the Future.* (Atlanta: John Knox Press, 1985).

Cooper, Kenneth H. and Mildred Cooper. *The New Aerobics for Women.* (New York: Bantam Books, 1988).

Corey, Marianne Schneider and Gerald Corey. *Becoming A Helper.* (Pacific Grove, CA: Brooks/Cole Publishing, 1993).

Covey, Stephen. *Seven Habits of Highly Effective People.* (New York: Simon and Schuster Trade, 1989).

Dale, Robert D. *Pastoral Leadership.* (Nashville: Abingdon Press, 1986).

Diehm, William J. *Sharpening Your People Skills.* (Nashville: Broadman & Holman: 1996).

Drakeford, John W. *The Awesome Power of the Listening Heart*. (Grand Rapids, MI: Zondervan, 1982).

Egan, Gerard. *The Skilled Helper*. (Pacific Grove, CA: Brooks/Cole, 1994).

Eisenberg, Ronnie and Kate Kelly. *Organize Yourself*. (New York: Collier Books, 1986).

Foster, Richard J. *Freedom of Simplicity*. (New York: Harper & Row, 1981).

Foster, Richard J. *The Challenge of the Disciplined Life*. (San Francisco: Harper & Row, 1985).

Gangel, Kenneth O. and Samuel L. Canine. *Communication and Conflict Management in Churches and Christian Organizations*. (Nashville: Broadman Press, 1992).

Hansel, Tim. *When I Relax I Feel Guilty*. (Elgin, IL: David C. Cook, 1979).

Helgesen, Sally. *The Female Advantage: Women's Ways of Leadership*. (New York: Doubleday Currency, 1990).

Hodnett, Edward. *The Art of Working with People*. (New York: Harper & Row, 1959).

Hunt, Susan. *Loving Leadership: Leader's Guide*. (Atlanta: Presbyterian Church in America, 1995).

Hunt, Susan and Peggy Hutcheson. *Leadership for Women in the Church*. (Grand Rapids: Zondervan, 1991).

Hutchins, David R. and Claire G. Cole. *Helping Relationships and Strategies*. (Pacific Grove, CA: Brooks/Cole., 1992).

Guinness, Os. *The Call: Finding and Fulfilling the Central Purpose of Your Life*. (Nashville: Word, 1998).

Jeffers, Susan. *Feel the Fear and Do It Anyway*. (New York: Fawcett, 1988).

Jones, Laurie Beth. *Jesus CEO: Using Ancient Wisdom for Visionary Leadership*. (New York: Hyperion, 1995).

Jones, Laurie Beth. *The Path*. (New York: Hyperion, 1996).

Keith-Lucas, Alan. *Giving and Taking Help*. (Chapel Hill: University of North Carolina Press, 1972).

Koestenbaum, Peter. *Leadership: The Inner Side of Greatness*. (San Francisco: Jossey-Bass, 1991).

Kraft, Vickie. *Women Mentoring Women*. (Chicago: Moody Press, 1992).

Krisco, Kim H. *Leadership and the Art of Conversation*. (Rocklin, CA: Prima, 1997).

Littauer, Florence. *Personality Plus*. (Grand Rapids: Fleming H. Revell, 1992).

Littauer, Florence. *Put Power in Your Personality*. (Grand Rapids: Fleming H. Revell, 1995).

McGinnis, Alan Loy. *Bringing Out the Best In People*. (Minneapolis: Augsburg Fortress, 1985).

Maloney, H. Newton. *Win-Win Relationships*. (Nashville: Broadman & Holman, 1995).

Maxwell, John C. *Developing the Leaders Around You*. (Nashville: Thomas Nelson, 1995).

Maxwell, John C. *Developing the Leader Within You*. (Nashville: Thomas Nelson, 1993).

Mayeroff, Milton. *On Caring*. (New York: Harper & Row, 1971).

Miller, Calvin. *The Empowered Leader*. (Nashville: Broadman & Holman, 1995).

Miller, Sherod, et al. *Connecting: With Self and Others*. (Littleton, CO: Interpersonal Communication Programs, Inc., 1992).

Minirth, Frank B. and Paul D. Meier. *Happiness Is A Choice*. (Grand Rapids: Baker Book House, 1978).

Porter, Carol and Mike Hamel (eds.). *Women's Ministry Handbook*. (Wheaton: Victor Books, 1992).

Rollins, Catherine E. *52 Ways to Build Your Self-Esteem And Confidence*. (Nashville: Thomas Nelson, 1992).

Sanders, J. Oswald. *Spiritual Leadership: Principles of Excellence for Every Believer*. (Chicago: Moody Press, 1980).

Sehnert, Keith W. *Stress/Unstress*. (Minneapolis: Augsburg, 1981).

Shulman, Lawrence. *The Skills of Helping*. (Itasca, IL: F. E. Peacock, 1984).

Stevens, Paul. *Balancing Your Life: Setting Personal Goals*. (San Jose, CA: Resource Publishers, 1996).

Wilkes, Gene. *Jesus on Leadership: Becoming a Servant Leader*. (Nashville: LifeWay Press, 1996).

Willard, Dallas. *The Spirit of the Disciplines*. (New York: HarperCollins, 1988).

Wilson, Robert A., ed. *Character Above All*. (New York: Simon and Schuster, 1995).

Worley, Karla. *Growing Weary Doing Good? Encouragement for Exhausted Women*. (Birmingham, AL: New Hope, 2001).

Also in the Woman's Guide series,

these Bible studies by Rhonda H. Kelley challenge women to deeper levels of spiritual health, holiness, and contentment. All studies contain twelve weekly lessons that are ideal for individuals or small groups.

N984104 • $12.99 • 1-56309-252-2

This workbook study guide of 12 weekly lessons based on Colossians reminds readers not to wait until there's a problem to monitor their spiritual health. Teaching guide included.

N004110 • $12.99 • 1-56309-432-0

Concise but thorough, this topical workbook study contains 12 weekly lessons to challenge women to lead a Christlike lifestyle. Teaching guide included.

N014110 • $12.99 • 1-56309-433-9

Contains astute biblical insights that challenge women to honestly examine their own hearts. Teaching guide included.

"Rhonda Kelley is one of the dearest women of faith I know. She is a gifted Christian communicator who lives what she teaches. She writes with the pen of Scripture and the ink of grace on the stationery of real life. You're going to love her!"
—**Beth Moore**, author of *Breaking Free*

"You will find penetrating challenges from Scripture and helpful tools for thoughtful introspection."
—**Dorothy Patterson**, Assistant Professor of Women's Studies, Southeastern Baptist Theological Seminary

"Rhonda Kelley writes with beautifully crafted words, engaging readers in understanding the Scriptures."
—**Esther Burroughs**, author of *Empowered!* and *Splash the Living Water*

Available in Bookstores Everywhere

New Hope Publishers

Equipping You to Share the Hope of Christ